Praise for
Why We Won't Talk Honestly About Race
(Previously titled *No Matter What . . . They'll Call This Book Racist*)

"No book I've read better captures the utter disingenuousness of America's racial politics over the past half century. Stein certainly will be called a 'racist,' which is why this book is so brave."

—Shelby Steele

"One of the best writers of our era, whose insightful new book, *No Matter What . . . They'll Call This Book Racist: How Our Fear of Talking Honestly about Race Hurts Us All* is a must read."

—Rush Limbaugh

"I sometimes hear from parents who have been appalled to learn that the child they sent away to college to be educated has instead been indoctrinated with the creed of the left. They often ask if I can suggest something to have their offspring read over the summer, in order to counteract this indoctrination. This year the answer is a no brainer: *No Matter What . . . They'll Call This Book Racist.*"

—Thomas Sowell, *The American Spectator*

"By the time you reach the final page, you will seriously wonder why the right has not had the courage to say this before; and, whether the right will, actually, ever have the courage to say it. In that regard alone, I give kudos to Stein who will almost certainly be attacked from all sides for putting this into print."

—Frank DeMartini, *The Hollywood Republican*

"A fearless writer like Stein and his new book constitute a bold, refreshing first step toward that 'frank conversation' that Eric Holder is so eager to have."

—Mark Tapson, *FrontPage Magazine*

"*No Matter What* is a fine book, and one that champions the earnest, positive message of lending a hand up rather than a handout."

—Joseph Cotto, *The Washington Times*

WHY WE WON'T TALK HONESTLY ABOUT RACE

Harry Stein

ENCOUNTER BOOKS • NEW YORK • LONDON

First American edition published in 2012 by Encounter Books,
an activity of Encounter for Culture and Education, Inc.,
a nonprofit, tax exempt corporation.
Encounter Books website address: www.encounterbooks.com

Manufactured in the United States and printed on
acid-free paper. The paper used in this publication meets
the minimum requirements of ANSI/NISO Z39.48–1992
(R 1997) (*Permanence of Paper*).

First paperback edition published in 2013.
Originally published in hardback in 2012 as: *No Matter What . . . They'll Call
This Book Racist: How Our Fear of Talking Honestly About Race Hurts Us All*.

LIBRARY OF CONGRESS CATALOGING-IN-PUBLICATION DATA
Stein, Harry, 1948–
Why we won't talk honestly about race/Harry Stein.
pages cm.
ISBN 978-1-59403-706-1 (pbk.: alk. paper)—ISBN 978-1-59403-707-8
(ebook)
1. United States—Race relations. 2. Americans—Attitudes.
3. Social psychology—United States. I. Title.
E185.615.S7236 2013
305.800973—dc23
2013007874

*To black conservatives everywhere,
shock troops in the battle
for America's soul*

CONTENTS

PREFACE

When this book was published in hardcover in the spring of 2012, it was entitled: *No Matter What . . . They'll Call This Book Racist*. Why is this, the paperback version, called instead *Why We Won't Talk Honestly About Race?*

The answer says almost as much about race and how we deal with it as anything in the pages that will follow.

The truth is, I struggled with what to call the book from the start. There are, of course, countless books out there on the subject of race, but I believed this one was saying things that were distinctive and even important, and it needed a title that reflected that, one that would give pause and perhaps even provoke. Midway through the writing, I hit upon one I thought might work. It was lifted from the famous sex book (and Woody Allen movie) of a few decades ago: *Everything You Always Wanted to Know About Sex**—with the asterisk reappearing at the bottom of the page—**But were afraid to ask*. Since one of the points of my book was that, on this most sensitive of subjects, even the most decent and fair-minded among us rarely risk saying anything that might give offense, my variation would read *Everything You Honestly Think About Race**, with the second part—**But are afraid to say*—serving, as in the original, as a kind of unexpected and amusing subtitle. While I suspected such a title might be seen by others involved in the title search as problematic, I thought that would be mainly because the book and film were so old that many contemporary readers would miss the joke. Instead, the resistance had to do with the words themselves; everyone with whom I conferred seemed to think that most would assume all those hidden, honest thoughts referred to in the title were, in fact, viciously, irredeemably racist.

As we went along, to one degree or another this proved to be a problem with almost every prospective title anyone proposed: there were lots of people out there ready, even eager, to misconstrue it. The list of discarded possibilities grew daily: 'Blackmailed'; 'Skin in the Game'; 'Affirmative Reaction'; 'The New Blacklist'. At one point my wife even put out the question to conservative/libertarian fellow thinkers on the Web, but they, too, came up empty.

At last, I hit on the notion of finding a title that would stick it to those whose reflexive condemnation we'd been so assiduously seeking to avoid: all those who deploy the racism charge as a blunt weapon to intimidate and silence. Or, as I like to think of them, the *real* race baiters. A slew of new ideas reflected this thought. While some were simple and direct ('The Racism Smear,' 'The Racism Lie'), and others mock-affronted ('Who Are You Calling Racist?,''Al Sharpton's NOT a Racist and We ARE?'), all displayed rich contempt for those who'd gotten away with playing the race card for so long.

The end result was the title that appeared on the original version of the book. All right, it was unwieldy, and, on first hearing, almost impossible to remember, but it seemed to make the essential point with a bit of humor and even panache. And in case there was ambiguity as to meaning, the subtitle— 'How our fear of talking honestly about race hurts us all'— would surely take care of that. (At the last minute, we did tweak the subtitle, replacing the more accurate 'terror' with the less daunting 'fear'.)

But, of course, it was all predicated on a miscalculation. I honestly—naively, stupidly, optimistically—believed that as a society we were very close to consensus on the reckless use of the racism charge; that, though it continued to be used with impunity by the academic left and some in the media, as well as for shamelessly political ends by black activists and craven liberal pols, no one with any sense was buying it anymore; that, to the contrary, with a black president in the White House, it was almost universally appreciated that the American people had made vastly greater progress on the racial front, and with far greater speed, than any other in history.

Then, a couple of weeks before the book was even out, the Trayvon Martin case exploded, and a lot of us watched with horror as the tragedy was exploited for ideological ends like none in recent memory. For weeks, a situation that was, at the very least, highly ambiguous, and quite possibly a legitimate case of self-defense, was furiously condemned by liberals everywhere as evidence that America remained deeply and irredeemably racist. Young Martin, so sympathetic commentators sadly intoned, echoing the crowds in the streets furiously demanding vengeance, was murdered for nothing more than the crime of being black. It was as if the past half-century had never happened. The case, so it was endlessly repeated, was a latter-day replay of the lynching of Emmett Till. George Zimmerman, himself a minority, was identified in *The New York Times* as a 'white Hispanic,' the tape of his panicked call to the local police that night inartfully edited by a major network to convey the false impression that he'd targeted Martin for the color of his skin. The victim, meanwhile, was portrayed as youthful innocence incarnate, just a good kid out one evening to pick up a bag of Skittles and a can of Arizona Iced Tea, rather than as the increasingly trouble-prone teen he was, under suspension from school at the time, who had allegedly been caught with a burglary tool. The Internet outrage and mass demonstrations only began to abate with the emergence of key facts—notably, that Zimmerman's version of events was largely confirmed both by his injuries and by eyewitness accounts. Not, true to form, that those who'd been heedlessly waving the bloody shirt of racism ever retracted their charges. As always, their only reaction after being exposed once again as having gotten things completely wrong, resembled that of Gilda Radner's Emily Litella on the old *Saturday Night Live*: "Never mind."

Alas, in the wake of the Martin case, reminders that the racism smear is as alive and intimidating as ever have continued to come in an endless, dispiriting parade. And what's especially telling is that even when the charge is utterly preposterous, it continues, as ever, to set off panicked denials. Take the ginned-up controversy that arose with the release of *Sports Illustrated*'s latest Swimsuit Issue. Since one of the photos of a bikini-clad babe showed her standing alongside an African bushman, the shot was seized upon as racist. As Columbia University's Marc Lamont Hill had it, it reinforced the crippling stereotype of Africans as "primitive" and "almost uncivilized." But rather than find a polite way to dismiss such critics as the idiots they are, *SI*'s public relations people immediately came forth with a groveling *mea culpa*, apologizing "to anyone who has taken exception to the way their culture was represented."

Then there was the case of the Caledonian Record, a newspaper in über-liberal Vermont, that made the mistake of supporting a local basketball team in its contest against archrival Rice by publishing a full page poster for fans to hold up at the game. In type suggestive of Chinese calligraphy, it read: 'Fry Rice.' In the storm that followed, the paper vigorously denied the racism charge, yet it also regretfully opined, in an editorial voice not unlike that of the hyper-sensitive men who populate NPR, that "the outcry reminds us that racial and ethnic stereotypes can offend— regardless of intent."

Think of it as a missed opportunity. Given the absurdities that abound on this issue, and the fact that there exists in contemporary America a racial pecking order nearly as rigid as the one that prevailed in the segregationist South, they might've made a far more important point by observing how much worse it could have been: for what if the rival school's mascot had been a chicken?

But also, needless to say, there have been plenty of more serious instances in recent days of the race baiters doing their dirty work. For instance:

Naomi Schaefer Riley, a key contributor to the influential *Chronicle of Higher Education*'s "Brainstorm" blog, was fired in response to complaints from the publication's readership, overwhelmingly comprised of academics. Her offense? A column on the lack of intellectual rigor that marks black studies programs on the nation's campuses. "Ms. Riley's blog posting did not meet *The Chronicle*'s basic editorial standards for reporting and fairness in opinion articles," the publication's editor piously explained, never mind that in posting so challenging a piece, (one saying out loud what many have long acknowledged privately), the writer was doing precisely what she'd been hired to do. ". . . As a result, we have asked Ms. Riley to leave the Brainstorm blog . . . I sincerely apologize for the distress these incidents have caused our readers and appreciate that so many of you have made your sentiments known to us."

A terrific writer, Riley can happily take care of herself. As she succinctly summed up the reasons for her dismissal in a *Wall Street Journal* piece, "black studies is a cause, not a course of study. By doubting the academic worthiness of black studies, my critics conclude, I am opposed to racial justice—and therefore a racist."

It might be worth noting, though Riley herself pointedly did not, that she is married to a black man, and her three children are half-black. Not that this would carry any weight with the race-baiters, since both she and her husband are conservatives, and thus denied the presumption of legitimacy that skin color otherwise confers. As a useful point of contrast, a few months later, the very liberal actor Alec Baldwin was also accused of racism, in his case for allegedly calling a bothersome black *New York Post* photographer outside his East Village apartment a "coon," a "crackhead," and a "drug dealer." But that story went largely unreported by the mainstream press, and Baldwin—who insisted he couldn't possibly be a racist, citing the fact that his foundation's last grant was $50,000 to the Arthur Ashe Learning Center—wasn't fired from any of his lucrative jobs or even reprimanded.

From her perch at MSNBC, talk show host and Tulane political science professor Melissa Harris-Perry let it be known that henceforth criticism of unmarried teen mothers should be considered out of bounds. Her outburst, received with enthusiasm in left-liberal precincts, was specifically directed at New York Mayor Michael Bloomberg, after the city launched a subway ad campaign aimed at clueing in young (and, yes, primarily minority) teens to the obvious: for a young girl to have a child is invariably to doom both to lives of profound distress. As one ad cogently observes: "If you finish high school, get a job, and get married before having children, you have a 98% chance of not being in poverty." That that message has not been sufficiently heard over the past five decades has everything to do with the tragedy that close to three-quarters of black children in America now grow up in homes without fathers.

But the ad campaign infuriated Professor Harris-Perry, who denounced it as an attempt to "blame young mothers for America's deepening poverty crisis rather than putting the blame where it belongs, on a financial system that concentrates wealth at the top and public policies that entrench it there."

One poster especially set her off. It showed a bawling black toddler alongside the words: "I'm twice as likely not to graduate high school because you had me as a teen." Raged Harris-Perry, "In a society that constantly tells black girls and women through popular culture and public policy that we are easily disposable, un-marriageable and wholly unlovable, this image of a child mocking her young mother with partner abandonment is a step too far."

What, of course, is truly a step too far for those like Ms. Harris-Perry is talking straight about teen pregnancy. It is not as if she really has anything against stigma, rather that, as always, she chooses to stigmatize those who seek to meaningfully address the tragic deficits associated with inner city culture.

But among the many liberal/left racial enforcers working so assiduously to keep a lid on potentially productive conversation, none has been quite so brazen lately as Philadelphia Mayor Michael Nutter, who reacted to a piece in a local magazine entitled 'Being White in Philly' with a call to essentially scuttle the Constitution.

By contemporary standards, the piece in *Philadelphia* magazine was indeed daring. Setting out to elicit the honest feelings
among white people about "the elephant in the room" issue of
race, reporter Bob Huber canvassed residents of the gentrify-
ing, middle class neighborhood of Fairmont. While the piece
is seasoned by more than a dollop of Shelby Steele's famous
'white guilt'—the interviewee with whom the reporter most
clearly sympathizes is a woman who bucked local group-think
to send her child to the overwhelmingly black neighborhood
school—he provides a diversity of views and voices, some of
them highly uncongenial to sensitive liberal ears. Almost all
the critics pointed to a woman identified as 'Anna,' the first
Fairmont resident quoted in the piece: "Blacks use skin color
as an excuse. Discrimination is an excuse, instead of moving
forward. It's a shame–you pay taxes, they're not doing anything
except sitting on porches smoking pot . . . Why do you support them when they won't work, just make babies and smoking pot?"

While such an observation is so commonplace it will surprise no one with a functioning set of eyes and ears—in the
privacy of their lives, people generally say what they mean and
don't worry what *The New York Times* thinks about it—it was
way, way too much candor for some.

So it was hardly surprising that the Mayor, who is black
and a conventional liberal Democrat, would be upset to see
such a thing in the pages of his local city magazine, or even that
he would term the piece "disgusting" and "pathetic"; while he
would have been mistaken, public officials are as entitled as
anyone else to be intemperate and hyperbolic. But His Honor
went far beyond that. In his official capacity, he dispatched a
letter to the city's Human Rights Commission, asserting that,
since free speech is "not an unfettered right," he wanted "the
Commission to evaluate whether the 'speech' employed in this

essay is not the reckless equivalent of 'shouting, "fire!" in a crowded theater,' its prejudiced, fact-challenged generalizations an incitement to extreme reaction."

It was, in short, the kind of outright abuse of governmental power that should have had liberals everywhere up in arms, especially those in the media. But, no, not in defense of a piece that dared, however tentatively, to move beyond conventional thinking on race.

Of course, that non-reaction surprised no one, for it is a given that the elite media have as long been in league in the great cover-up on race as the politicians they favor. "At the heart of the left-liberal ideology that dominates American debate about race is a glaring contradiction," as the *Wall Street Journal*'s James Taranto observed of the episode. "In theory, white attitudes toward blacks are all-important, in that any difficulties blacks experience are said to be the result of white racism. But as we have seen with Mayor Nutter's reaction to Huber's article, there is no interest in pondering *actual* white attitudes toward race, and every interest in suppressing—or stereotyping—them."

But what for so many of us is every bit as distressing as the profound dishonesty of liberals on race is that so many of those on the other side of the political spectrum continue to timidly concede them the moral upper hand.

This is a phenomenon amply discussed in the pages of this book. But it is worth noting that since the publication of the hardcover, the GOP has blown yet another great opportunity to meaningfully set itself apart on the issue.

I speak of the 2012 presidential campaign.

In Barack Obama, Mitt Romney found himself with a rival whose actions and policies had been an even more colossal disappointment on the racial front than in other respects. Indeed, the election of the man who many in 2008 had hoped and believed would serve as a one-man antidote to America's long and terrible history of racial division had instead resulted in greater ill feeling between the races than at any time in recent memory, as key administration figures, not excluding the President, had repeatedly played the race card to demonize perceived opponents. While Attorney General Eric Holder shamelessly took the lead in this regard, even managing to cast attacks on his department's calamitously bungled Fast and Furious gunrunning scheme as motivated by his and the President's race, other Obama appointees, like former 'green jobs czar' Van Jones and FCC 'diversity czar' Mark Lloyd, were not far behind. The President himself, while more measured, likewise needlessly stirred the racial pot, weighing in on highly volatile situations before the facts were in, and always endorsing the familiar liberal narrative of white culpability and black victimhood. Harvard Professor Henry Louis Gates's 2009 arrest for attempting to break into his own home prompted a precipitous presidential declaration that the Cambridge police had "acted stupidly," with Mr. Obama citing "a long history in this country of African-Americans and Latinos being stopped by law enforcement disproportionately." Even worse was the President's pointed observation, as the fury over the killing of Trayvon Martin was reaching a crescendo, that "if I had a son, he would look like Trayvon." Delivered wholly out of context, on the occasion of the appointment of the new head of the World Bank, the remark could only serve to enflame, as indeed it did, that already volatile situation.

Nor were such episodes out of character. Even while Mr. Obama presented himself as a uniter in 2008, his reflex was to cast the other side as eager to exploit America's none-too-latent racism. "We know what kind of campaign they're going to run. They're going to try to make you afraid," Obama warned. "They're going to try to make you afraid of me. He's young and inexperienced and he's got a funny name. And did I mention he's black?" Even Bill Clinton, hitherto accorded honorary status as America's first black president, found himself targeted during the heat of the 2008 primaries, noting in astonished indignation that Obama was "playing the race card on me."

Taking the hint, in his run against Obama that year, John McCain steered so clear of race that he'd become furious if any of his supporters dared mention his rival's longtime intimate association with the notorious racial arsonist Jeremiah Wright.

Unfortunately, like McCain, Romney was in the gutless tradition of the modern GOP on race, so the likelihood of his ever seriously addressing the issue in 2012 fell somewhere south of the odds that the Mets would win the World Series. Lest we forget, this was a guy who refused to even take on Obamacare.

A strategist's dream, Romney paid absolutely top dollar for absolutely the worst possible advice. So when it came to race, his handlers played it strictly by the book. Knowing that the media would endorse any charge by Obama that his rival's bringing up race was more evidence of Romney's, and his party's, not-so-latent racism, they urged what they always do: caution.

And it was true, of course, that had Romney dared speak out in unexpected ways on the subject he'd have been eviscerated. Early on, as if to send a warning shot across his rival's bow, the President suggested to Spanish-language Univision that Romney supported racial profiling, and, soon after, one of the President's chief media enthusiasts, Chris Matthews, felt free to blithely refer to Republicans as "the Grand Wizard crowd." Other mainstream liberals were soon repeating the fiction that Republicans are adept at 'dog whistle racism,' subtly communicating to white voters a shared antipathy toward blacks in general and, in particular, the black man in the White House. When Romney delivered an economics speech in Ohio before a banner reading "Obama isn't working," the liberal blogosphere pounced, one indignant columnist at Mediaite fuming it called to mind "the stereotype of the 'lazy,' 'shiftless' black man." Meanwhile, media outlets across the board were broadcasting reminders that Romney's church did not admit blacks to the priesthood until 1978.

So, throughout the campaign, Romney remained dutifully silent, never addressing the lamentable state of the nation's inner cities or the cultural deficits that have so much to do with it; or America's epidemic of children growing up without fathers and the desperation and lawlessness that will be visited upon the nation as a result; or the profound inequity of racial preferences; and certainly not that this president, who'd pledged to unite us, has instead endlessly dwelt on past injustices long since remedied, while further empowering the racial bean counters who hold such sway in the nation's life.

Would taking on Obama on this most crucial and dangerous of subjects have made a difference electorally? Hard to know. What is certain is that Americans have a keen sense of fairness; polling consistently reveals that we believe in equal opportunity and a level playing field, that no one should be either penalized or privileged by race or ethnicity. Most of us know full well that racial discrimination is no longer the obstacle to life success that liberals relentlessly, and often cynically, claim.

But, yes, Romney would have been pummeled by the press and would have aroused Bush-Cheney levels of detestation among the elites.

But he'd at least have shown himself capable of something he so conspicuously failed to display during the long months of the campaign: leadership.

In a roundabout way, this brings us back to the original title of this book and why it is no more. Yes, from the beginning I realized it would put off some liberals, and that was okay, because my hope was that it would elicit curiosity and the occasional smile from conservatives and libertarians, its intended audience. Instead, it seemed to put off, or at least rattle, most who saw it, and to be misunderstood by just about everyone else.

It is hard enough for a book out of a small conservative house to draw notice in a crowded marketplace. A title that very few want to get caught reading in public doesn't help. This hit home with particular force during the promotional phase. I've been writing for a long time, and this was my first book ever for which I was not asked to do a single minute of TV.

So think of this new title, bland as it is, as a nod to McCain, Romney, and the ignoble GOP tradition of safety at all costs. But forget the packaging. For any 'progressives' out there looking to be offended, there's still the content.

INTRODUCTION

Before I wrote even a word of this book, a number of people who wished me well suggested I drop the project. They knew the kind of books I'd done in the past, and of my tendency to kid around in print, and they suggested that in this instance that would be a very, very bad idea. As one bluntly put it, "You don't make light about race in this country."

That was not my intention, I countered. My aim was to talk *honestly* about race, conveying views that, however legitimate or widely held, have been effectively branded as racist by defenders of the lamentable status quo, and so largely banned from public discourse. Indeed, the book's original title was drawn from the famous Tea Party sign first spotted, as far as I can discern, in the hands of an anonymous witty soul at a 2009 rally in Cincinnati: "It Doesn't Matter What This Sign Says, You'll Call It Racist Anyway."

And, by the way, what's wrong with a little irreverence on the subject? After all, there are those who make light about race all the time. Richard Pryor built a whole career on it, and so have dozens of his successors and imitators, more than a few of them wildly profane.

Okay, I got it: What my solicitous friends meant is that *white people* can't make light about race. Or, for that matter, say things in deadly earnest that violate the ever-evolving rules of what is permissible. And that holds especially true for white conservatives.

I sincerely appreciated it all—I too live in the world of Al Sharpton and the *New York Times*, if only at its margins—but their concern also provoked a question: *Why not?* Aren't the issues surrounding race, from the social fallout of single-parent families to the ways racial preferences distort the very meaning of equity and justice as embodied in the nation's founding documents, of concern to us all? Moreover, hasn't the impulse to ignore or justify or even celebrate behaviors that once would have been everywhere condemned as dysfunctional led to the collapse of standards generally? As a reformed white liberal I can say with complete assurance that white liberals share many of the same concerns, even if they'd be mortified to be overheard voicing them among strangers.

Quite simply, the fear and unspoken prohibitions that have long governed the conversation about the single most important issue on the public agenda have served only to undermine genuine progress on the racial front.

And the time has come to move past that.

There are of course deeply compelling reasons that as a subject race is the extremely sensitive and awkward thing it is. As the historians aptly have it, slavery was America's "original sin," and in the century to follow, even second-class citizenship was a status denied to most of the nation's blacks. The very terminology associated with the era—"separate but equal," "poll taxes," "lynching"—bespeaks a nightmarish state of affairs all but incomprehensible to the contemporary mind. It is wonderfully good (and quite remarkable) that, though that time was so recent that tens of millions living today vividly recall it, we almost universally look back upon it with shame and even incredulity.

But shame is a psychologically complex thing, and never more so than when applied to Americans and race. For even as it has impelled us to examine our ugly past with unflinching honesty—with every elementary school kid nationwide versed in the horrors of the Middle Passage, and slave narratives all the rage with history grad students, and black oppression the *leitmotif* of every Ken Burns documentary—it has precluded anything approaching an honest view of race today; indeed, it has much to do with why such honesty has itself been routinely cast as racist.

No one has written more compellingly about this deeply dispiriting phenomenon than the brilliant Hoover Institution scholar Shelby Steele. Since Steele is a conservative—and a black one, at that—people who read publications like the *New York Times* have mostly never heard of him, but he nailed the source of their racial attitudes more succinctly than anyone in the two-word title of his most important book: *White Guilt*. It is the widespread guilt over the terrible inequities of the past (and to a lesser extent, the obvious hardships faced by many blacks in the present) that causes white people, especially those who identify themselves as "enlightened" or "progressive," to over and over, *ad infinitum*, give blacks a pass on behaviors and attitudes they would regard as unacceptable and even abhorrent in their own kind. This guilt has repeatedly, in fact, induced liberal whites—and even some not so liberal— to embrace policies that institutionalize not fairness but its opposite so as to appear to be on the right side of the racial divide. "The great ingenuity of interventions like affirmative action," Steele writes, "has not been that they give Americans a way to identify with the struggle of blacks, but that they give them a way to identify with racial virtuousness quite apart from blacks."

Each of us, of course, has his own unique set of experiences with race, but having come of age during and in the immediate aftermath of the civil rights movement—that is, believing, as the Reverend Martin Luther King Jr.'s most fundamental precept had it, that we should be seen as individuals rather than as members of a group—I suspect the ones that inform this book are representative of a great many well-intentioned Americans. That is why I raise Steele right up top. The moment I read him on white guilt, I experienced what certain feminists have taken to calling an "ah-ha moment." I was in my late 30s at the time and, no question, he was describing not just me but pretty much every well-meaning white person I had ever known: All of us who had gone lazily along with the mainstream liberal racial flow.

Good intentions. These have long been the currency in which liberal whites have traded, and where race was concerned, the family into which I was born boasted some of the best. Though by the time I was aware of such things my parents were Stevenson Democrats, they had been Communists, and remained proud of that fact (though for a time secretly) the rest of their lives. And in good measure—indeed, this is a large part of the romance of the left in general—it was because in the twenties and thirties the Communist Party *was* way ahead of the curve on the big social issues: fighting (and incessantly sloganeering) against poverty, sexism and especially racism. Nor was this merely a theoretical or tactical pose. For instance, it was CP lawyers who led the fight to save the Scottsboro Boys, the nine hapless black teens unjustly accused of raping a pair of white girls in Depression-era Alabama. My mother for a time worked as the secretary for James Ford, the black former postal worker who in the thirties twice ran for vice president on the Communist ticket. Decades later, she would tell us of hearing the stories of indigent blacks who'd journeyed to New York from the rural South to tell rapt young Communists of taking their lives in their hands organizing their fellow sharecroppers. "There was one fellow," she recalled, and I have this verbatim, because I got it on tape before she died, "who looked like the Hollywood stereotype of what a Negro should look like, very black, huge ears, white teeth—like Stepin Fetchit. But this man had such dignity! I never forgot what he said about this dual life he had to live: 'The only reason I'm alive today is that down South I shuffle, I say, Yassush, yas m'am.' Otherwise, he said, they'd have lynched him a long time ago. It made such an impression on me!"

And when my parents told such stories, they made quite an impression on my two brothers and me, too, as did what we heard from our more progressive teachers. My fourth-grade teacher in particular, the wonderful Mrs. Levin, talked ceaselessly about prejudice. She'd have us sing "You've Got to Be Taught" from *South Pacific*, and her rendition of the poem "Incident," by Countee Cullen, had such a powerful effect on me I can still recite it by heart more than 50 years later.

Once riding in old Baltimore,
Heart-filled, head-filled with glee;
I saw a Baltimorean
Keep looking straight at me.
Now I was eight and very small,
And he was no whit bigger,
And so I smiled, but he poked out

His tongue, and called me, "Nigger."
I saw the whole of Baltimore
From May until December;
Of all the things that happened there
That's all that I remember.

Still, by then my father had a successful career going in capitalist America, we were living in an affluent, all-white neighborhood in suburban New Rochelle, and the only two black kids in my elementary school were the sons of the United Nations ambassador from Ghana. So my brothers and I couldn't help wonder sometimes: *What's going on here?* Because pretty much the only Negroes our family had anything to do with on a day-to-day basis were the ones who worked for us—Edward, who did occasional odd jobs around the house and drove my older brother to Little League practice, and the various young women from the South who were our housekeepers. Among these, we grew especially fond of one who stayed a couple of years with us when I was approaching my teens. Her name was Del, and one evening my older brother and I, partly to be pains in the ass, but also because we meant it, began pressing our parents about her. Why was it that she was "Del," while they were "Mr. and Mrs. Stein"? Why, for that matter, did Del serve us dinner, but never sat with us at the table? In their youth my parents had picketed *Gone with the Wind* for its portrayal of black people in general, and the black servants in particular, and it was clear this line of questioning made them extremely uncomfortable, which was highly gratifying. But to my mother's credit, she at least tried to formulate coherent answers. That wouldn't be the kind of relationship Del wants either, she said, such familiarity would make *her* uncomfortable. When we went on to press them about Del's salary—if memory serves, less than a hundred dollars a week—she argued that that was the going rate, in fact *more* than the going rate, and infinitely more than she could make down South, and let's not forget she also got room and board.

At that point, we relented. It was fish in a barrel and just too pathetic.

Listen, I don't want to overstate this—both my parents are gone now, and can't defend themselves. And no one can doubt their *good intentions*. For in this regard, as in many others, my liberal parents truly were par for the course. Just about everyone we knew had a black maid, which is surely why within their circle their small hypocrisies were so rarely challenged. This is not to say that the young black women living inside those large white homes were ever demeaned or mistreated. To the contrary, many were almost members of the family—emphasis on *almost*. The family of one of my friends had a "girl" named Willie Mae—it always made me think of the great center fielder for the Giants—who stayed with them for decades, so couldn't really have been a girl at all. Nor, apparently, was it all that different even in parts of the country where most people's parents regarded Communists with roughly as much sympathy as did Joe McCarthy. Alabama-born Howell Raines, the deeply unpleasant individual who would go on to become the top editor of the *New York Times*, wrote a 1991 piece for the paper's Sunday magazine about what he had learned of life as a child from his family's devoted black maid. His "early relationship with Grady," as Raines later recalled, "prepared me for the civil rights story and made me receptive to it perhaps in a way many white Southerners might not have been." The piece won a Pulitzer Prize, and it may truly be said that, in all the long history of that degraded award, none was ever more of a gimme. (It is somehow—what's the word: fitting, ironic, unsurprising?—that the ever-smug Raines would ultimately lose his vaunted *Times* post in the wake of the Jayson Blair plagiarism scandal for having tolerated in a black reporter practices that would have led to instant dismissal had he been white.

Still, mixed as Raines's motives surely were, his enthusiasm for the civil rights movement was certainly genuine, for it was the great moral crusade of all our young lives. As a 14-year-old, in 1962, I joined the Congress of Racial Equality (CORE) to do my bit, which consisted of occasionally picketing the speaking appearances of alleged racists, but more often of getting together to hold hands with other young activists to sing songs like "Down By the Riverside" and "We Shall Overcome"; and it was exhilarating to believe we were connected to the earth-shaking events unfolding every evening on TV in places like Mississippi and Alabama. My father, for his part, actually flew down to Alabama to take part in the final leg of King's legendary Selma to Montgomery march.

As it happened, we had our own mini-civil rights crisis in my hometown of New Rochelle, precipitated when a cohort of parents at the all-black Lincoln School insisted that the city, instead of erecting a new building for their elementary school-aged kids, bus them to the all-white schools in the better parts of town. The National Association for the Advancement of Colored People soon came aboard on their behalf, and the battle lines were drawn: the black parents, the NAACP and their liberal white allies, including us, versus the other white parents, whose arguments for preserving the neighborhood school system we naturally brushed aside as cover for racism. In short, it soon got ugly, literally neighbor against neighbor. In the end the fight went all the way to the Supreme Court, where the busing advocates at last prevailed. By then I was in high school, long gone from the schools in question—and within a system where, ranked by academic merit, kids like me rarely had more than a couple of Negroes in our classes. But stories of the newly integrated elementary schools were everywhere being spread by wide-eyed younger siblings, a fair number of whom were regularly getting the crap beaten out of them by their new classmates.

Still, as good liberals, who had time to dwell on actual consequences? We were caught up in the grand sweep of history, *change*, even when it was just for its own sake.

Actually, the rough stuff wasn't nearly as much a surprise to us kids as it seemed to be to our parents. Though we'd been raised to believe Negroes were like us in every vital respect— why else would you have to be carefully taught to love and hate?—somewhere along the way we'd come to grasp that some of them weren't *exactly* like us. I'd personally figured this out back when I was eight or nine, and our parents would drop us off Saturday afternoons at the movies on Main Street. More than once, I was accosted at the soda machine by black kids demanding, with a show of menace, to "borrow" a quarter. The first time this happened I remember thinking, in my naiveté. *Borrow? But we don't know each other, so how will you pay me back?* But I was quickly led to understand that was not the transaction they had in mind. Relatively painless as those encounters were, at the time they were pretty scary. I mean, there were some crummy kids in our neighborhood—chronic liars, cry babies, bullies, and fools—but no actual robbers!

Not that I ever bothered to tell my parents. I must've understood on some level that while I'd get some sympathy, there'd be no satisfaction, and I might have to endure an "explanation"—a suburban version of the young Woody Allen's father's defense of the cleaning woman caught stealing in *Annie Hall*: "She's a colored woman from Harlem! She has no money! She's got a right to steal from us!"

In any case, in the immutable way these things happen, I came to share their understanding that, having been so deeply wronged by history, black people were always to be given the benefit of every doubt. By the time I was in college, Vietnam may have been atop the agenda as an animating campus issue, but race was not very far behind. Like every other right-thinking white kid, I seamlessly went with the new direction dictated by posturing black activists. Sure, King had been fine in his day, but that day was done—now it was Stokely Carmichael, H. Rap Brown, the Panthers, and all the other strutting Black Power types who commanded our awed respect, even if (and maybe also because) they scared the hell out of us.

Of course, later we would come to recognize that all along they'd been pretty thuggish, but that was also only when everyone else did, and it was safe to do so. Anyway, by then there were new positions to be taken on the racial front, like, for instance, supporting black studies and affirmative action and otherwise pushing *diversity* in its assorted and nefarious forms.

I only began to question—no, actually, *think* about—any of it when I began moving to the right; a move prompted by a number of things, not least becoming a father. It was around this time that, exploring an intellectual universe into which I'd otherwise never have dared venture, I ran across the aforementioned Shelby Steele, among other conservative thinkers. In due course, I joined them in questioning my own long-held liberal assumptions in print, eventually doing so at book length.

Only then did I come to fully understand how dangerous such apostasy could be, especially when it came to race. I've written the story before, so I'll be succinct. While giving a speech about my political journey in Dallas, I made a light reference to how in my family we used to root for sports teams based on how many blacks were on the roster; then compounded this misdemeanor with a Class-A felony by closing the speech with a story about an argument between my 15-year-old son and his politically correct white high school

English teacher over *Adventures of Huckleberry Finn*. Pointing to Mark Twain's strategic use of the n-word, the teacher claimed, to my son's exasperation, that this classic of anti-racist literature was racist, and when he took her on, he guaranteed, as he put it, that "I'm starting off with a C in that class, and working down from there." Except in telling the story I made the mistake—which I will not repeat here, so as not to give other idiots easy ammunition—of using not the weasel term "the n-word," but the actual word itself. This grievously offended a black man in the audience, who rose during the question and answer portion of the program to say so. We had a spirited back and forth, and I thought that was the end of it. Except that he, or one of his friends, immediately went to the local *Fort Worth Star-Telegram* with a grossly distorted account of the episode, which led to a grossly distorted article coming as close as legally feasible to calling the "conservative speaker"—me—a racist; and in due course, the story was picked up by a number of other papers.

Actually, as these things go, the gruesome experience ended reasonably well. After I wrote about it in *City Journal*, a *Wall Street Journal* columnist followed up, leading to a gratifyingly high number of people to cancel their subscriptions to the Fort Worth paper, and I choose against all odds to believe the liberal writer of the piece and his even more liberal editor were duly chastened. But for all my subsequent bravado, it was a searing experience and one I would only wish on my worst enemies—which, since they're all liberals, is wishing for the impossible.

What's ironic about being branded a racist at this point in life is that, in fact, I have more and better genuine black friends than ever before. True enough, they're almost all on my side of the political spectrum—but, hey, isn't friendship most fundamentally about shared beliefs and values?

All of this background is by way of lending context to all that will follow; and, yes, I suppose also as a means of rebutting some of the ugliness likely to come.

The ways in which this book will be anathema to the racial enforcers are many and varied. Start with double standards—the kind that may also be filed under "liberal-white bigotry," i.e., the bigotry of low expectations, and how it cripples and demeans those it supposedly aims to help. It will look into the supposed sin of racial profiling—and the statistical evidence establishing that, in fact, the disproportionate arrest and incarceration rates of minorities usually reflect nothing more than disproportionate rates of criminality. Too, it will discuss how American business has long been subject to blackmail by the racial grievance industry in the name of social justice; as well as the many other ways in which the regime of racial preferences has sowed division, corruption, and resentment in this country.

Speaking of double standards, nor can the role of the media be discounted in any of this. How is it okay for liberals to endlessly belittle Clarence Thomas as an Uncle Tom, or for liberal cartoonist Ted Rall to get away with calling Condoleeza Rice a "house nigga"? Why, even after the Duke University rape fiasco, does the media continue to give credence to every charge of racism?

But beyond the manifold particulars, I aim to make a larger and overarching point: The idea that it is racism that has millions of underclass blacks mired generation after generation in physical and spiritual poverty is not just false, but the greatest impediment to fundamentally altering that dreadful state of affairs. What must be faced—above all, by its victims—is that the real problem is a culture of destructive attitudes and behaviors that denies those in its grip the means of escape.

Alas, rather than fully confront the all-too-obvious deficiencies of underclass culture, we play an elaborate, multifaceted game of let's pretend; one that begins with the fiction that racism is the all-encompassing explanation for black (and other) social dysfunction and moves on seamlessly to the fraud that even the most soul-crushing anti-social behaviors can constitute "authenticity."

In the end, comforting lies are no better than any other kind—arguably worse, for being so seductive. Societies that invest too heavily in them invariably reap the whirlwind. (See former Soviet Union's Five-Year Plans or Greece circa 2012.)

In brief, this book aims to unequivocally say the sorts of things that for too long have been deemed unsayable in the public square—even when widely acknowledged in private among Americans of goodwill. Its intent is not to offend or shock, though it will likely do both, but to provoke the sort of serious thinking that liberal enforcers have heretofore rendered impossible; and by facing up to those difficult truths, to begin looking toward genuine solutions.

For all the remarkable progress this country has made on race in the past half-century, unprecedented in human history, liberals insist, for their own political and psychological purposes, on clinging to the notion of America as irredeemably racist. We—and especially black people—for too long have been living with the terrible consequences of that cruel canard.

This gets us back to where we started. One friend took me out to lunch to warn me off this book: It's career suicide, he assured me, if not the regular kind. I'd get savaged, *massacred*— scalped, castrated, my body burned to such an unrecognizable crisp that no one but my dentist and that gorgeous forensic anthropologist on *Bones* will be able to identify it. Hadn't I noticed that in the Age of Obama, the racism charge, rather than abating, has become more prevalent than ever?

Yes, I've noticed.

I'll confess that did give me pause. So let me conclude, for safety's sake, with a comment with which I wholeheartedly agree made by a reader called Extraneus on the excellent JustOneMinute website: "For the record, I have no problem with Obama's black half. His white half is the most incompetent, anti-American asshole ever to inhabit the office of the presidency, but his black half is fine."

RACISM TODAY, RACISM TOMORROW, RACISM FOREVER

For many of us who grew up during the civil rights movement, Alabama Governor George C. Wallace was the vilest figure in the rogues gallery of Southern bigots blighting the nation. True, Mississippi Governor Ross Barnett was for a time equally obstructionist, but he had the look and milquetoast manner of an accountant. While thuggish Public Safety Commissioner Eugene "Bull" Connor of Birmingham, Alabama shocked evening news watchers nationwide by siccing attack dogs on peaceful protesters, he was so stupid and oblivious he seemed less a multidimensional human being than a pot-bellied racist sheriff out of a Herblock caricature. But Wallace—the former bantamweight fighter, chin outthrust in snarly defiance as he stood literally blocking the schoolhouse door—was smart and canny and utterly self-assured; which is to say, he seemed the embodiment of all that was ugly not just in America, but in humankind itself.

Wallace's June 1963 refusal to allow two black students to enter the hallowed halls of the University of Alabama was the fulfillment of the infamous pledge he'd made at his inauguration five months earlier. Standing at the precise spot where Jefferson Davis took the oath of office as president of the Confederate States of America a century before, he declared, "I say segregation today, segregation tomorrow, segregation forever."

So despicable was the thinking represented by that pronouncement that for millions of Americans it will forever remain Wallace's epitaph; this, despite his late-career disavowal of racial bigotry and his strong support from black Alabamians in his last campaigns. In fact, in retrospect Wallace was a complicated and even a tragic figure, in many ways representative of the lightning-fast transformation of the Old South to the New South. (Hardly incidentally, he anticipated the mass disillusionment with traditional liberalism that would lead to the wholesale exodus of working-class whites from FDR's New Deal coalition and the rise of Reagan Democrats.) I myself, very much later, came to appreciate his bizarre yet somehow apt characterization during his 1968 presidential campaign of the liberal elites as "pointy heads who can't park a bicycle straight." But that's another matter.

It was the indelibility of Wallace's earlier racism, expressed as it was with such callous and intractable certainty, that made a declaration by Detroit Mayor Kwame Kilpatrick more than 40 years later so startling. Appearing at an NAACP dinner on April 30, 2006, in the middle of a campaign launched by affirmative action opponents for a Michigan state proposition aimed at ending government racial and gender preferences in education and hiring, the mayor pledged: "Affirmative action today, tomorrow, and forever."

Ultimately, Kilpatrick and his allies were unsuccessful, as that November Michigan's Proposal 2 passed overwhelmingly.

Nor did the mayor himself fare any better: Charged three years later with 10 felony counts of corruption, he resigned his office, and for a time found himself federal inmate No. 44678–039.

But what's far more significant is that among his fellow liberals his eerie, repulsive echo of Wallace elicited absolutely no criticism. To the contrary, hearing it, his NAACP listeners erupted in cheers; and they, too, went without censure in the press and elsewhere. Indeed, campaigning at Kilpatrick's side in 2008, then-presidential candidate Obama bestowed upon him a particularly heartfelt helping of boilerplate, declaring him "a leader, not just here in Detroit, not just in Michigan, but all across the country people look to him. We know that he is going to be doing astounding things for many years to come. I'm grateful to call him a friend."

Welcome to the wide world of civil rights activism in a time when all the meaningful battles have long since been won. Which is to say, an activism that—largely for purposes of reaping liberal support and government dollars—tirelessly promotes the fraud that today's version of racism constitutes a moral crisis nearly on a par with the virulent kind once represented by Wallace.

Which brings us to Eric Holder.

One will recall that on February 18, 2009, less than a month into Obama's supposed "post-racial" presidency, U.S. Attorney General Holder commemorated Black History Month by declaring the American people "essentially a nation of cowards" for not talking more about race. "If we are to make progress in this area," he piously intoned, "we must feel comfortable enough with one another and tolerant enough of each other to have frank conversations about the racial matters that continue to divide us."

This was so utterly, indisputably, laughingly wrong that those of us not reduced to outright mockery were left flabbergasted.

Too little discussion of race? Race has long been our national obsession, a pastime more widely followed than football—which, in fact, itself regularly gives rise to mini-racial conflagrations—or Oprah Winfrey (who's never averse to fanning the conflagrations). Liberal commentators refuse to shut up about race; college students have it pushed in their faces from the first day of orientation on through to the *de rigueur* pieties about "diversity" and "social justice" at graduation; of necessity, most every Fortune 500 company has instituted policies aimed at hiring and promoting minorities, and woe be to recalcitrant managers who too adamantly adhere to more traditional standards of merit.

Seemingly each day we must endure some new illustration, large or small, of the ludicrous lengths to which this insanity has gone. Hall of Fame quarterback Warren Moon charges *Pro Football Weekly* with racism for describing up-and-coming star Cam Newton, a fellow black, as "very disingenuous" and "very scripted" with a "me-first" attitude—never mind that the publication had used exactly the same words to describe spoiled white players. According to the tabloids, "many" believed that *So You Think You Can Dance* judge Mia Michaels was a racist, based on her decision to vote AdéChiké Torbert from the show. (Not to worry: A distraught Michaels defended herself by revealing she has dated black men.) Even the lunatic at a Connecticut beer distributorship who gunned down five co-workers after getting fired for theft cried racism, claiming he'd been subject to racist taunts.

As national obsessions go, this is quite a bizarre one, since most of us, left to our own devices, would prefer to take those we encounter in life as they come, on the merits In many cases we would scarcely notice race at all if it were not for the fact that we are constantly being harangued about it by our progressive betters. Indeed, as Ann Coulter put it in one of her more spot-on observations, "Liberals and white supremacists are the only people left in America who are neurotically obsessed with race."

Happily, white supremacists have largely gone the way of the dodo. Liberals, on the other hand, remain all too much with us, daily wielding the racism charge with all the subtlety of a caveman's club.

Is there still white racism out there? Absolutely, there remains a scattering of genuine unreconstructed bigots hanging out in the damp cracks and crevices of the sub-basement of the grand American edifice, embarrassments to themselves and the human species. Every critic of the racial status quo readily acknowledges as much, if only in preemptive self-defense.

Then, again, one's answer to the question depends upon one's definition of the term. What most of us see, and celebrate, is how little there remains of the old kind, the cretinous Wallace kind, in which millions—and even the law—defined others as loathsome or inferior based on the meaningless superficialities of ethnicity and race. Today, the vast majority of Americans, almost all of us, embrace King's admonition to judge others solely by "the content of their character."

Yet many liberals will tell you the term carries a broader meaning—that it also has to do with what's in people's hearts, what we say behind closed doors. On the face of it, this view sounds reasonable enough, and it deserves its fair-minded due. For instance, to summon up perhaps the most obvious manifestation of such supposed racism, it is true that lots of white people tell racist jokes, including many who would never think of repeating them in front of a black person, and, for that matter, plenty of liberals.

Recently heard examples:

What do you call a white man surrounded by 100 black guys? Warden.

What do you call a black hitchhiker? Stranded.

True enough, in the spectrum of ethnic jokes, these are on the relatively mild side—many are frankly noxious—and, also true, they are grounded in an unpleasant stereotype about blacks and criminality. And, yes, we'd probably be better off if they never got told—as liberals will surely legislate if they can get away with it. Indeed, having grown up in a scrupulously left-of-center home, I recall being shocked at some of my supposedly enlightened college friends' love of *The Amos 'n Andy Show*; my own childhood must-see TV ran from *Leave It to Beaver* to *Wagon Train*. Yet listening to them recall certain beloved episodes—like the one in which the shyster Kingfish sold the credulous Andy a "house" in Central Park that was a stage backdrop, so you went through the front door and were outside. I must say, stereotypes and all, they sounded pretty damn funny.

Call it racism if you want—by the broadest definition, maybe it is—but, if so, it's the most benign sort of racism. Does it even need to be said that we also tell mean and ugly jokes about Poles and Italians, women and transvestites, Southerners and blondes—most based on exaggerations of presumed characteristics? I'm not exactly delighted by non-Jews telling Jewish jokes that feature penny pinching or the Holocaust. (For example: How do you get 100 Jews into a car? Toss a dollar bill inside. How do you get them out again? Mention Hitler is driving.)

But this is the price of living in a multiethnic society that places maximum value on freedom; one that also lets middle-aged women parade around in T-shirts that ask "Who Needs Big Tits When You've Got an Ass Like This?" Hardly incidentally, as a means of acknowledging difference, and maybe of letting off steam, it has it all over the simmering ethnic hatreds so common elsewhere in the world.

Is it channeling Pollyanna to suggest that even Holder might be well served by spending as much time celebrating how far we've come as he does on our supposed cowardice? Not long ago, catching *Guess Who's Coming to Dinner* on TV, I was reminded that a mere 40 years ago the notion of a white woman marrying literally the most accomplished black man in America would've been considered shocking even by an exceedingly liberal San Francisco couple like that played by Katharine Hepburn and Spencer Tracy. These days, Sidney Poitier's Dr. John Prentice—rushing off from a high-level conference in Hawaii to an even more prestigious one in Geneva, making even the words "What's for breakfast?" sound like Shakespeare—would be a catch in almost any household anywhere in America. Nor is it a surprise that 2009's best loved film, resonating like no other, was *The Blind Side*, about the love of a conservative, upper-crust Mississippi family for the black man-child they took in as their own.

In a society that decades ago reached a consensus that legal discrimination is an abomination, and has grown in innumerable other ways as a result, one can choose to be endlessly aggrieved about the incidental stuff. Or, quite simply, not be. Alas, far too many black people, as well as legions of white liberals, have opted for the former, embracing a definition of racism so expansive that almost anything—from the failure of too few blacks to pass an exam for promotion to a perceived slight at a social function—can be made to fit the bill.

Think of it as chip-on-shoulder racism, a.k.a., the kind that can never end; the all-purpose explanation and excuse. What's continually curious, given the hyper-sensitivity of such people to the merest hint of racial bigotry, real or imagined, is how blithely indifferent they are to racial animus when it is directed at white people by blacks. White America was stunned when it learned of Obama's longtime association with the vile Jeremiah Wright during the 2008 campaign, but what's just as telling is that in the south side of Chicago, the odious black liberation theology on offer to Wright's 8,500-strong congregation at Trinity United Church of Christ was not seen as a big deal; for variations on the same doctrine are heard in black churches each Sunday in many parts of urban America. Indeed, just sticking to Obama's hometown, in today's America can anyone even imagine a white equivalent of unhinged racial rabble rouser Louis Farrakhan garnering so remotely large a following?

In fact, throughout black America can be found those with a considerably less-than-generous view of white people, one grounded in the assumption that no matter the face they present to the world, on some level most are irredeemably racist. Whether expressed in anger or bemusement or resignation, there is no hesitation in airing such a view, and certainly no embarrassment. It's just how things are. Nurtured by the omnipresent grievance industry, a pervasive sense of resentment and ill usage cuts a wide swath across educational and class lines, as evident in a black dorm at an elite university as on any street corner in urban America; and informing the thinking of many educated and successful blacks very nearly as much as that of Wright or Farrakhan. As David Mamet perceptively has his upper-crust black lawyer put it to a white colleague in his play *Race*: "Do all black people hate whites? Let me put your mind at rest. You bet we do."

That may be an overstatement, but it is inevitable that the incessant message that racism lurks at every turn would breed distrust and deep antipathy toward white people among many in the black community.

While the O.J. Simpson verdict may have been the most striking instance of black solidarity trumping justice, the cogent observer of modern America will not be entirely surprised to learn it is not the only one; or that these days black racists are likely to be a good deal more candid about their biases than their white counterparts. In fact, I have before me a story from the *Pittsburgh Tribune-Review* about a black judge in the Pittsburgh area who recently rejected a plea agreement for a white man with no priors convicted of scuffling with a cop after a traffic stop. From the bench, Allegheny County Judge Joseph Williams called the deal "a ridiculous plea that only goes to white boys," adding that "if this had been a black kid who did the same thing, we wouldn't be talking about three months' probation." The shocked assistant district attorney on the case, rightly noting that "the court has essentially called me a racist," protested "I don't make offers based on race. I make offers based on facts."

It is not coincidental that among Holder's other notable early acts was his astonishing decision to *drop* a case, which was against members of the New Black Panther Party who'd intimidated white voters at a Philadelphia polling place, that his predecessors at the Department of Justice had already won. Though Holder never offered a plausible reason for this, it is entirely consonant with the lunatic theory, which is nonetheless advanced by seemingly serious people, that blacks *cannot* be racist by virtue of their experience as victims of racism and lack of institutional power.

But whites? In the eyes even of some blacks who themselves wield vast institutional power, the behavior of white people is always presumed to be governed by deep-seated racism. "I do not understand what I think is the maligning and maliciousness [toward] this president," as Texas Congresswoman Sheila Jackson Lee complained bitterly during the contentious negotiations on raising the debt ceiling in the summer of 2010. "Why is he different? And in my community, that is the question that we raise. In the minority community that is [the] question that is being raised. Why is this president being treated so disrespectfully?"

The questions leaping to mind were enough to leave one sputtering in stupefied frustration. *Disrespect?!* Wasn't the partisan sniping Barack Obama faced just par for the course in such a circumstance? Was she actually pretending to have forgotten George W. Bush, or that she herself sought to have him impeached? Why was race being dragged into this already bitterly divisive matter at all?

Indeed—as long as she dragged it in—had she truly not noticed that Obama, woefully unprepared for the job though he was and increasingly revealed in office as scarily inept, had long been uniquely *protected* from anything approaching routine scrutiny by virtue of his race?

I remember picking up the *Amsterdam News* back in the early eighties, when Ed Koch was New York's mayor, and being shocked by the none-too-subtle insinuation in a publication generally regarded as respectable and mainstream that the white (Jewish) mayor had it in for the city's black residents simply on the basis of race. As the lauded black novelist James Baldwin titled a famous 1967 essay, without irony (and, indeed, in justification of such a view): "Negroes Are Anti-Semitic Because They're Anti-White."

Obviously, no decent soul would have expressed that sort of contempt for black people even then. Yet in September 2010, (to light upon a particularly blatant recent example), the *Village Voice* ran a cover story titled "White America Has Lost Its Mind." Basically a rehash of the by-then standard trope (though one accepted as fact in much of black America) that cast all opposition to Obama's agenda as racist, it attracted significant attention for its, shall we say, vigor of expression. Its author, black staffer Steven Thrasher, claims such opposition "seemed to have taken root deep in the lizard part of the white nervous system . . . the lies and distortions of the rat-fuckers are being soaked up by the damaged crania of this country's drooling white masses. What sort of senility is softening up the frontal lobes of America's palefaces that they can't see through the black hatred of a wanker like (Andrew) Breitbart? . . . Is there any hope? Can the white mind be cured? And what—other than a massive lobotomy—can salvage it? It's hard to imagine a cure when, at this point, the patient doesn't seem to realize that he's sick."

Roger Ebert pretty much summed up the reaction of white liberals to the piece with his tweet: "Just got around to reading 'White America Has Lost Its Mind.' Pulls it all together and makes sense."

Why does black racism, unlike the white kind, get away with it scot-free? Why does even something as odious as the flash mobs of wilding black teens that in recent years have terrorized Milwaukee, Denver, and Chicago, among other cities, targeting *only* whites and Hispanics for robbery and brutal beatings go largely unremarked upon by the media and society at large? Because the elites who decree cultural norms (and once did so with a fair amount of rigor) today bring to any matter involving black behavior a toxic mix of condescension and excuse making. Black people are not the same as us, so the implicit thinking goes, and given their tragic past, it is not just reasonable but understandable that they not be held to the same standards.

Of course, occasionally unavoidable, an especially high-profile instance of anti-white bigotry will cause a serious stir. The Reverend Jesse Jackson gave rise to much hand wringing in left-liberal circles when he was caught on tape in 1984 referring to New York as Hymietown. And then there was Wright, the *plus ultra* in black racial demagoguery.

Yet even in such cases, the denouement is predictable. A lot of anguished commentary, followed by explanations/apologies and the earnest determination to put it all behind us. In brief, the usual double standard on especially vivid display.

What too rarely gets observed is how profoundly damaging this endless nursing of resentments is to blacks themselves in alienation from the American mainstream, or the incalculable damage the victim mind-set does to race relations in general.

Then, again, for some, it is damage with a purpose, and the costs more than justify the reward. For it is also only the specter of racism that keeps in business a civil rights establishment long since given over to economic and moral corruption. The NAACP and other "social justice" outfits need the racism charge every bit as much as in their day the George Wallaces and Ross Barnetts needed the bugaboo of integration: as a means of holding and exercising power. They depend for their very existence on the perpetuation of the notion that white racism in its varied and nefarious forms remains the overriding impediment to minority progress, and so must be confronted via the expenditure of bottomless amounts of government cash and corporate capital until the source of the vile inequity ceases to be or the end of time, whichever comes last.

That over the years they've exploited the charge to the fullest is a melancholy matter of public record. Indeed, with the actual white racists of old happily a distant memory, they've had remarkable success in endlessly conjuring up new ones, largely imagined and always exaggerated.

It hardly needs to be said that the masters of this debased art are Jesse Jackson and Al Sharpton. But among white progressives, Morris Dees and his colleagues at the Birmingham, Alabama-based Southern Poverty Law Center, or SPLC, surely lead the pack. Ostensibly "dedicated to fighting hate and bigotry, and to seeking justice for the most vulnerable members of our society" by "monitoring hate groups," the SPLC is a veritable fund-raising behemoth, forever sending out ominous warnings as fund-raising appeals to its massive list of credulous supporters. Alas, as Mark Krikorian writes in the *National Review Online*, with the all-but-nonexistent "Klan an increasingly improbable stand-in for the SA,"—Hitler's brownshirts—"the SPLC needed new enemies to keep the cash registers ringing. So, after the collapse of the Bush/Kennedy/ McCain amnesty push in 2007, it joined with [the National Council of La Raza and other open-borders groups that wanted to effectively criminalize disagreement with their positions to find new 'hate groups' among immigration skeptics, designating the Federation for American Immigration Reform as a 'hate group. . . . Who will be the next 'hate group'? The Catholic Church? The Southern Baptist Convention? The Orthodox Union? Or maybe they'll go after Second Amendment groups next, or anti-tax groups, or the anti-Islamists." In fact—no joke—it turned out the next group to make the list was the Family Research Council, deemed a "hate group" for its opposition to gay marriage. Hey, if you're going to "claim in fund-raising letters that there's been a 54 percent increase in the number of hate groups since 2000," as conservative columnist Ashley Herzog observes, "you do what you have to do."

Yet by far the most fruitful instrument in the racial extortionist arsenal in recent decades has been the concept of "institutional racism," a term invented by Carmichael in the late sixties, which he defined as "the collective failure of an organization to provide an appropriate and professional service to people because of their color, culture, or ethnic origin." The beauty part, of course, is that it is *organizations*, as opposed to mere individuals, that are to be held responsible for the racism and made to make restitution; a circumstance that no one has exploited with greater gall than Jackson, dubbed with endless justification the Godfather of Shakedowns. Among the many organizations that over the years have shown the "civil rights icon" their neck, and thanked him for the privilege, are Toyota, Viacom, Ameritech, Anheuser-Busch, and Coca-Cola.

Meanwhile the NAACP, routinely accorded the respectful designation as "America's most venerable civil rights organization" by the mainstream press, has repeatedly resorted to gutter tactics to pass for relevant, tossing out the racism angle with disgraceful abandon. It might well have hit bottom with its ad during the 2000 presidential campaign accusing candidate George W. Bush of complicity in the 1998 murder of a black man named James Byrd Jr. by three white men. "On June 7, 1998, in Texas my father was killed," intoned Byrd's daughter in the ad, which ran the final week of the campaign. "He was beaten, chained, and then dragged three miles to his death, all because he was black. So when Governor George W. Bush refused to support hate-crime legislation, it was like my father was killed all over again."

Nor was it coincidence that Bush's rival, Al Gore (who in the 1988 Democratic primaries unearthed Willie Horton and used him to beat up rival Michael Dukakis before George H. W. Bush did so in the general) chimed in on the NAACP's behalf. "James Byrd was singled out because of his race in Texas, and other Americans have been singled out because of their race or ethnicity," Gore piously intoned during the second presidential debate. For, needless to say, a relationship between the civil rights movement and the Democratic Party that at its inception was largely grounded in high principle has long since been reduced to a corrupt bargain; the race baiters posing as champions of social justice receiving legitimacy and consistent infusions of public money in return for assured and overwhelming black electoral majorities.

What's surprising, and deeply disheartening, is how intimidated even otherwise principled conservatives have invariably been by the threat of being branded racist. When accused of racial insensitivity of any kind, the impulse of many on the right has been to retreat in panic and confusion, slavishly apologizing or claiming to have been misunderstood or misquoted.

To be sure, the reasons for such feckless behavior are varied and complex. For some, it is at least partly driven by the recognition that having often been on the wrong side of the civil rights movement when it counted, conservatives must now make a point of their commitment to inclusion; Barry Goldwater, for one, who opposed the landmark civil rights bills of the mid-sixties (on principled if, he later decided, mistaken states rights grounds), spent much of the rest of his career doing a kind of penance.

But more often, preemptive surrender—or invisibility—on race-related issues is just easier for conservatives than taking on the massed forces of civil rights orthodoxy. This is, of course, understandable: Who the hell needs the media questioning your racial *bona fides*, which is to say, your very morality? Still, to be MIA on an issue of such incalculable importance to the nation's well-being is not just a gross abdication of responsibility, it lends credence to the charge at the very heart of progressives' worldview that, in contrast to their profoundly decent selves, those on the right are callously indifferent to the plight of the underclass.

It hardly need be said that the racism charge remains a particular problem for conservatives from the Deep South. When Mississippi Governor Haley Barbour was considering a presidential run in early 2011, the *Weekly Standard*'s Andrew Ferguson asked the prospective candidate why his hometown of Yazoo City had been spared the racial violence suffered by other Southern towns. Barbour gave what seemed like a reasonable response. "You heard of the *Citizens' Councils*? Up north they think it was like the KKK. Where I come from it was an organization of town leaders. In Yazoo City they passed a resolution that said anybody who started a chapter of the Klan would get their ass run out of town."

But, of course, "up north" is where the history of the civil rights revolution is written and revered, largely by those who know of it secondhand, and in the accepted version the White Citizens' Councils were themselves among the era's chief villains, bitter obstructionists in suits and ties, instead of in white robes bearing nooses, as one liberal pundit had it. On the other hand, Barbour was there, and the town had been peaceful, so he presumably spoke with some authority. Still, inevitably, the media pounced, making much of his evident unconcern for intolerance—both then and, presumably, still. The firestorm "lasted 72 hours or so, during which he went from plausible and respected presidential prospect to the subject of an *Economist* story with the death-rattle headline 'Is Haley Barbour Racist?'" later observed Ferguson, the best writer on contemporary media behavior going. He added that "I had a good vantage on Barbour's descent because I wrote the article that got him into so much trouble. No, that's not quite right: better to say, I wrote the article that was read by the people who used it to get him into so much trouble."

Inevitably, Barbour quickly issued a statement of clarification: ". . . My point was my town rejected the Ku Klux Klan, but nobody should construe that to mean I think the town leadership were saints, either. Their vehicle, called the *Citizens' Council*, is totally indefensible, as is segregation. It was a difficult and painful era for Mississippi, the rest of the country, and especially African Americans who were persecuted in that time." Soon after, Barbour chose not to make the race, and who can blame him?

The truth of what actually occurred in Yazoo City back then? It didn't matter.

More than one leading Republican has deluded himself in recent years that the way for Republicans to square themselves with the black community, and thus break the Democrat hammerlock on the black vote, is to embrace affirmative action and the other aspects of the multicultural agenda as enthusiastically as those on the other side. Ken Mehlman, the Republican Party's national chairman during Bush's second term, was especially keen in this regard. While his stance led to praise from the *New York Times*, which lauded him for having repeatedly "apologized for what he described as the racially polarized politics of some Republicans over the past 25 years" and for "what civil rights leaders view as decades of racial politics practiced or countenanced by Republicans," it didn't exactly have the desired effect on voters, black or white. In 2006, for example, when a highly controversial initiative to ban affirmative action was on the ballot in Michigan, Mehlman pushed the GOP's gubernatorial candidate, Dick DeVos, to oppose it. The result: in the face of a powerful Democratic tide nationwide, the anti-affirmative action proposition passed 58 percent to 42 percent—the same percentages by which DeVos lost, while garnering the standard sub-10 percent of the black vote. An object lesson of what happens when caution morphs into outright cowardice.

Hardly incidentally, support for the Michigan anti-preference proposition came from voters across the political spectrum, as had also been the case when similar measures appeared on the ballot in other blue states such as California and Washington. According to exit polls in the latter, for instance, while 80 percent of Republicans supported I-200, so did 62 percent of independents and 41 percent of Democrats.

In short, standing up to the racial bullies of the left, in addition to its other considerable virtues, is a clear political winner. And how could it not be, in a nation that in overwhelming measure still holds fast to the ideal of taking others as individuals rather than as members of a group, and judging them solely on the merits; and that thirsts for honesty on the subject of race?

Indeed, the most pernicious consequence of the left's incessant depiction of well-meaning Americans as driven by racism may be the chilling impact it has had on the no-holds-barred conversation on race that we need to have; one that would look unflinchingly at the culture of dependency and how it undermines the self-reliance and independence of mind that have traditionally led to success in this culture.

Of course, that's precisely the conversation the civil rights establishment and liberal Democrats are most anxious to avoid. "The definition of a racist today," as radio host Chris Plante observes of their most effective means of making sure we don't have it, "is anyone who is winning an argument with a liberal."

Indeed, what was most telling about Holder's invocation of American racism was its timing. After all, this was understood everywhere to be a celebratory moment—more, a *historic* one. Events having not yet revealed Obama as a left-wing partisan and well-tailored empty suit, his election was being widely lauded as proof we'd forever left the worst of our past behind. Even many of us who'd seen through him from the beginning, and shouted ourselves hoarse to friends and relatives too smitten to see, were pleased with what his election said about the citizens of this great land: That easily bamboozled as we Americans can be, we are not bigots. That, indeed, though parts of our country abandoned legally sanctioned bigotry a mere two generations ago, we have embraced true racial tolerance— which is to say, *indifference* to skin color—more fully than any other people on Earth.

Yet it is clear now that this is not the message Obama and his circle took from this election, and certainly not the one they wished to see Americans in general embrace. For the world as they see it to make sense, racism must be ever-present as a root cause, the all-purpose explanation for every problem faced by minorities in America. In fact, the very *last* thing Holder wants is a serious examination of why, in this freest and most prosperous of nations, so many minorities continue to lag economically and educationally, or why rates of criminality in the inner cities are so appallingly high. What the Obama factotum—whose department would in short order turn the very idea of justice on its head by enforcing only those voting rights cases in which minorities were the victims—was after was a fresh reading of the old indictment, with its too-familiar bill of particulars. As the estimable Heather Mac Donald enumerates several of the chief counts: "Police stop and arrest blacks at disproportionate rates because of racism; blacks are disproportionately in prison because of racism; blacks are failing in school because of racist inequities in school funding; the black poverty rate is the highest in the country because of racism; blacks were given mortgages that they couldn't afford because of racism."

For those who cling to the agenda of today's rotting hulk of a civil rights establishment, the possibility of losing racism as an issue—i.e., as a weapon—is intolerable, provoking the Pavlovian reaction of ginning up the rhetoric about how America remains an unremittingly racist nation, indifferent if not outright hostile to anyone not born to fair skin and privilege. Their mantra: "Racism now, racism tomorrow, racism forever!"

As his department began setting policy in the racial arena, Holder aimed, at the very least, to put his opponents on the defensive. Certainly, there seemed to be no downside. After all, for the liberal opinion makers and trendsetters who set themselves up as America's social-justice referees, the reaction to any such invocation of racism, past or present, personal or institutional, has always been deeply respectful—anyone thus accused, even if it's an entire population, is presumed guilty of at least *something*.

Decades of liberal control of the race conversation in America have had basically the same result as Dear Leader Kim Jong-il's brutal rule over the North Korean populace; what is permitted to be said is so ingrained, and the consequences of transgression so severe, that approved behavior is self-enforced. My friend Ward Connerly, long the leader of the fight against racial preferences, once observed that he's had the experience more times than he cares to count of speaking before an audience and knowing that 99 of 100 people agree with him. "But if there's one angry black person in the audience who disagrees," he said, "that person controls the room. He'll go on about the last 400 years, and institutional racism, and 'driving while black,' and the other 99 will just sit there and fold like a cheap accordion." And Connerly is black himself.

In his autobiography, Connerly tells another story that serves to remind that a full decade before Holder's empty call for a more honest national conversation on race, another Democratic administration struck the identical theme. Bill Clinton's version of that conversation, dubbed "One America in the 21st Century: The President's Initiative on Race," was announced in a speech to the graduates of University of California, San Diego in June 1997. Its aim was to promote dialogue "in every community" in America. To this end, Executive Order 13050 set up an advisory panel on race, headed by the ardently liberal, "distinguished" black historian John Hope Franklin and including six others—also "distinguished" and liberal. The panel soon hit the road, holding town meetings and university conclaves throughout the country, looking for and invariably finding evidence that racism remained rampant. So stacked was the deck that even some in the media began to remark on the panel's absence of ideological (if not ethnic) diversity. As a result, Clinton belatedly convened a White House conclave of prominent conservatives on the front lines of the racial debate in America. Among these was Connerly.

This is where the story gets interesting. As Connerly describes the meeting, Clinton was his usual eager-to-please self, alternately gregarious and earnest, and otherwise making every effort to appear open to his conservative guests' views. But Vice President Gore, sitting beside him, openly seethed. While Connerly, who had recently gained national recognition leading the successful fight for passage of California's anti-affirmative action Proposition 209, was certainly accustomed to hostility, he was taken aback to encounter such naked loathing in such a setting. Always exceedingly civil with opponents, he tried to engage the vice president but without success. But it was Gore's farewell that left the strongest impression. As Connerly describes it, after a cordial word of farewell from the president, he turned to Gore. The vice president grabbed his hand, "but instead of shaking it, he ground my palm and fingers in his grip as hard as he could. I felt the cartilage compress and almost cried out in pain. I looked at the vice president and he stared back at me with a slight smile as we walked out."

Think of Gore as the very embodiment of advanced liberal thought (as indeed he thinks of himself proudly), and it makes a kind of horrific sense. For of course the aim of the racial Torquemadas is to crush free inquiry, especially if it involves innovative thinking from the right; and, whenever possible, to destroy reputations and careers along the way. Ask Newt Gingrich, who, in the wake of the 1994 Republican landslide that would make him House Speaker, famously broached the subject of orphanages as a possible means of salvaging the lives of inner-city welfare children doomed to lives of degradation and criminality. The reaction in the "child-advocacy community" was as immediate as it was predictable. Gingrich wanted "to take children away from their parents just because they are poor," declared a spokesman for the National Coalition for Child Protection Reform, while "pro-child" activist Joan Criswell wrote that "What Willie Horton was to Bush, the teenage welfare mother is to the Republican proponents of the Contract with America." For its part, the mainstream press was little short of giddy at having been handed such a gift. "The party that professes to support family values seems excessively eager to yank poor children away from their mothers and dump them in institutions," mocked the editorialists at the *New York Times*. *Time* magazine, also harping on "the proposal's obvious incompatibility with 'family values,'" was just one of the big-time outlets to summon up the term "Dickensian"; while *Newsweek* saw the new "Republican revolution" already slipping "toward enfizzlement." The "idea of putting children into orphanages because their mothers couldn't find jobs," piled on Hillary Clinton, was "unbelievable and absurd," and a few days later her husband devoted his weekly radio address to the subject. "There is no substitute—none—for the loving devotion and equally loving discipline of caring parents," he intoned. "Governments don't raise children; parents do."

Gingrich briefly stood his ground, declaring he couldn't "understand liberals who live in enclaves of safety who say, 'Oh, this would be a terrible thing.'" But when he suggested that perhaps his opponents should take a look at the vintage Mickey Rooney orphanage film *Boy's Town*, the mockery reached new heights, with presidential advisor George Stephanopoulos snickering that if Gingrich was looking for a work of fiction as a model, a far more useful one would be *Oliver Twist*.

Within days, Gingrich threw in the towel. Yet even now, at the very mention of the word "orphanage," liberals rush to recall Gingrich and his misbegotten scheme. Indeed, it is a testament to how committed they remain to their discredited worldview that 27 years later—27 years that have only exacerbated the intractable problems of underclass Americans—another out-of-the-box Gingrich suggestion (that child labor laws might be modified to help imbue underclass kids with the work ethic so clearly absent in their communities) was greeted with equal scorn. NBC's David Gregory spoke for many of his colleagues in denouncing the idea as "grotesque," while others summoned up Ebenezer Scrooge and—who else?—Oliver Twist.

All of which brings us back to the attorney general's fantastical—and calculated—call for honesty on race. In its wake, something funny started happening—something Holder and his boss and the hordes of professional race baiters in government, academia and the media never counted on: Lots of us have stopped playing along. There was more than a hint of it during the brouhaha over Henry Louis "Skip" Gates, the Harvard professor and presidential friend who in the summer of 2009 had a meltdown when cops stopped him trying to break into his own Cambridge home. Gates's reflex to proclaim himself a victim of racism—and, Obama's, to endorse that view, without so much as a wisp of evidence—turned the incident into the "teachable moment" the president declared it to be. But what it taught was not, as from long experience they had every reason to expect, that bigotry and police maltreatment of minorities thrive even in supposed bastions of tolerance and inclusion like Cambridge, but that instantly jumping to such a conclusion is itself *prima facie* evidence of a distorted worldview; and, more, that even the most blameless and forward-looking whites (for in this case, the accused cop had an exemplary record of service and racial sensitivity) can suddenly find themselves in the crosshairs of the racial enforcers. For here was Obama himself, so famously cautious and deliberative it took him months to choose a family dog, making it all too clear that, facts be damned, on this issue, the former community organizer wholeheartedly embraces the black victim/racist cop trope as fully as does the loathsome Al Sharpton.

Before it was over, even casual news followers understood that the very phrase "teachable moment" was a liberal dodge, hauled out whenever a prominent liberal gets into a serious fix involving race, and dutifully echoed by a compliant press. Lest we forget, Obama's previous "teachable moment" had come at the low point of his presidential campaign, with the revelation that the man he'd embraced as his spiritual advisor regularly spouts the vilest kind of hateful tripe.

But the recognition that the racism trope was starting to lose its terrible power really took hold as the Tea Party movement came into prominence. Suddenly liberals were making the charge more promiscuously than ever, aiming it not at skinheads living in their parents' basements or at would-be Klansmen, but at decent Americans with the temerity to object to presidential policies they believed damage both the quality of their lives and the nation itself: in short, at Americans acting in the best tradition of democratic citizenship. This was, pure and simple, as George Will observed, "McCarthyism of the left—devoid of intellectual content, unsupported by data . . . a mental tic, not an idea but a tactic for avoiding engagement with ideas."

Indeed, when a 2008 *Los Angeles Times/Bloomberg* poll reports that a mere 3 percent of Republicans (as opposed to 4 percent of Democrats) would refuse to vote for a black man for president, the charge was so obviously preposterous, and profoundly offensive, that literally millions who'd never before given the matter any thought could not but take notice. And what they saw is what has long been true: That the accusation of racism is almost invariably a crock—and that more than just an expression of (often contrived) liberal moral outrage, it's intended to be the ultimate conversation stopper. As the conservative essayist and blogger Timothy Dalrymple aptly observed, "The accusation says more about the accusers than the accused."

As Hollywood might say, this is the great reveal of Obama's abortive "post-racial" candidacy and presidency. Early on, by virtue of his calculatedly moderate presentation, Obama seemed to a very great many to be precisely the idealized black leader (and, more, representative black *man*) that whites of all political persuasions yearned for in a national leader, someone who fully embraced, along with other traditional middle-class attitudes and values, their time-tested understanding of justice and fairness, and so would at last put an end to the racial divide. Instead we got an administration more recklessly promiscuous in its misuse of the racism charge than any in living memory. As cartoonist Bruce Tinsley had his cartoon duck reporter Mallard Fillmore mockingly intone at the height of the liberal attacks on Tea Partiers: "In other news, the Democratic National Committee has issued a recall of millions of race cards. . . . In a statement released yesterday, they admitted that while the cards had worked reliably for half a century, they have become worn-out and ineffective . . . and may blow up in users' faces."

Talk about unintended consequences! Through sheer overuse, the most potent weapon in the liberal racial arsenal is today increasingly ineffective. The result is that at long last there exists at least the possibility that Americans can begin to have the essential conversation on race that our "candor-phobic elites," in Andrew C. McCarthy's wonderfully felicitous phrase, have so long ruled beyond the pale; the one that moves beyond the self-serving pieties of contemporary liberalism to focus on the actual causes of—and even address—the intractable social and economic dysfunction so widespread in parts of the black community.

Think back on the Gingrich orphanage episode. In retrospect, what's especially telling is that the idea may well have had considerable merit. Haphazardly tossed into the public arena as it was, and lacking in definition, it was a starting point for what might have been a highly original policy initiative with the potential to salvage many young lives. What's worse is that more than a few of those on the other side, including the Clintons, surely recognized that—yet they attacked and belittled anyway, not only to rack up easy political points but to play to a key element of the Democratic base. Why? Precisely *because* implicit in Gingrich's proposal, as in others put forth by those seriously interested in addressing the failure of generation after generation of the underclass to grasp America's brass ring, was a fundamental challenge to the nefarious, all-consuming fiction. That is to say, the understanding that it is not the color of their skin that minimizes the life chances of inner-city kids, or even their undeniably difficult economic circumstances, but the culture into which they are born; from the near-certainty they will grow up fatherless to the attitudes they are likely to internalize about education and hard work to general chaos and lack of order in their homes.

It goes without saying that your basic liberal will take such a frank assessment, or even more equivocal musings along the same lines as—what else?—racism. Yet what's so odd about that is that *everyone* knows it's true. The reality of black inner-city life is inescapable in contemporary America, common knowledge, as evident on network TV crime shows, and the stand-up routines of black comics as in the impenetrable sociological studies turned out by mirthless academics. For all that, racial activists and their liberal allies have long managed to see to it that anyone with the temerity to raise the matter of values or behavior in a policy context is marginalized.

But now, at long last, in the Age of Obama all that can start to be discussed. You want to talk irony? As once, two generations back, George Wallace enabled a long overdue national conversation about the evils of segregation, so Barack Obama is making possible the conversation he surely never wanted about race.

MEDIA ENABLERS AND OTHER RACE MONGERS

Will someone please answer me this? How in the name of all that is good and decent did the self-promoting racial hustler *par excellence* Al Sharpton ever get to be respectable? So much so he was handed his own TV show on an NBC outlet?

No, just kidding. Foolish question, because it's all too clear: We're talking nearly three decades of mainstream media enabling. Actually, there's a kind of frightening logic to it. The media has treated Sharpton with kid gloves all these years because, in the end, the view he so tirelessly promotes—of an irredeemably racist America, in which black people's failures are more society's fault than their own—is one they share.

Quite simply, whether in ignorance, ideological blindness or simple fear, the media, ever fixated on the racism angle, has doggedly refused to face the harder truths of race in America. Indeed, an excellent case can be made that it is in the racial arena, more than in any other, that its distorted worldview has done the most grievous harm.

For in giving credence to Sharpton and other preachers of victimhood, and otherwise buying into the America-as-oppressor narrative, the media mandarins do more than merely salve their liberal consciences; they do their considerable bit to perpetuate a belief system that undermines literally millions. For a community to accept victim status, as for an individual, is to accept the presumption that effort is futile. Such a presumption not only saps energy and initiative, it *justifies* it.

This is what makes the case of Al Sharpton so revealing. Think of him as the fat, loud-mouthed canary in the media's tunnel vision: If it is possible to overlook a history as poisonous as his, *anything* could be overlooked. Why not portray Bernie Madoff as merely a charming rogue? Why not Charlie Manson as just another misunderstood romantic rebel? Why not also give David Duke his own show?

The damage Sharpton has done to this country's well-being is inarguably greater than any of them.

As far back as 1987, Sharpton was covering himself with disgrace as one of the chief perpetrators of the notorious Tawana Brawley hoax, wherein a 15-year-old upstate New York girl falsely claimed to have been abducted and raped by six white men. Acting as one of her three advisors, Sharpton inflamed passions by naming an assistant district attorney as one of the supposed attackers, and claiming authorities were protecting him and the others because they were white. Once the evidence proved Brawley had been lying in order to avoid telling her stepfather she'd been with a boy, the assistant D.A. sued and was eventually awarded $345,000 from Sharpton and the others for defamation of character. But to this day, Sharpton has never had the decency to apologize.

Four years later, when a seven-year-old black child was tragically run down by a car driven by a Jew in Crown Heights, Brooklyn, Sharpton again barged onto the scene, staging a rally where he called Jews "diamond merchants" and proclaimed, "If the Jews want to get it on, tell them to pin their yarmulkes back and come over to my house." In the four days of riots that followed, Jews were beaten in the streets and one was stabbed to death by rioters shouting, "Kill the Jew."

Four years after that, in 1995, Sharpton helped lead a boycott against a white-owned store in Harlem, publicly denouncing its owner as "a white interloper." Soon afterward, one of the protesters, thus incited, busted into the store, shot four employees and set the place ablaze. The final toll was seven dead.

Over the years since, he has continued to exploit, and worsen, virtually every racially charged incident in the New York area, as well as many far beyond. A mere listing of names of tragic black shooting victims—Amadou Diallo, Ousmane Zongo, Sean Bell—is enough for many to recall the flames onto which Sharpton has hastened to pour fuel. Moreover, he has continually been in trouble with the IRS for failing to pay his taxes.

Yet, for all this, he is not only treated with seriousness and respect by the mainstream media, but is routinely accorded the status of "civil rights leader." He is always among the first called upon for his views on all racial matters and is even allowed without challenge to pass judgment on the racial *bona fides* of others; for instance, declaring Mitt Romney unfit for the presidency by virtue of his Mormonism and urging that Rush Limbaugh be banished from the airwaves for racial insensitivity. "You've got to remember that those stations that Rush Limbaugh is on and others are regulated by FCC, granted by FCC; they go back to them to get waivers," he intoned in November,

2010. "They have the right to set standards. That does not impair your right to speak what you believe, but it does say that you are not going to do that to offend groups of Americans based on their race, their gender, their sexual status—none of that."

Even when the media passingly acknowledges Sharpton's many past indecencies, it is by way of claiming he has "grown." "Take a look at Reverend Al," as Lesley Stahl put it in a glowing *60 Minutes* report, ". . . stately in his tailored suits, commanding a national stage." Yes, Sharpton has gone through "a metamorphosis," the former "street-protest agitator" emerging as "trusted White House advisor, who's become the president's go-to black leader, campaigning around the country for President Obama and his agenda. Today, Reverend Sharpton looks and sounds like a totally different person."

More than merely respectable, he is embraced as a lovable, larger-than-life character whose excesses, such as they were, are readily dismissed as inconsequential. Even before MSNBC gave him his own show, the Internet Movie Database, which lists appearances by actors and celebrities in films and television, had no fewer than 10 single-spaced pages of appearances for Sharpton, almost all as "Himself." While most were as a guest on political or late-night chat shows, or on documentaries like *Obama: The First 100 Days* and *Moonwalking: The True Story of Michael Jackson*, many were variety shows or sitcoms. He has hosted *Saturday Night Live* and been featured on the *Tony Awards*, shown up on *Boston Legal*, *Law & Order: Special Victims Unit*, and *My Wife and Kids*, and made cameos in such films as *Mr. Deeds* and *Cold Feet*.

Of course, it is easy to shrug this off as media business as usual; we all know the media is biased across the board, and has a soft spot for lovable scoundrels, as long as they're on the left, and even more so if they're members of "underrepresented minorities." As conservative columnist Joe Sobran memorably summoned up the ultimate *New York Times* headline: "NEW YORK DESTROYED BY EARTHQUAKE: Women and Minorities Hardest Hit."

Still, the extraordinary indulgence the media has long shown to the loathsome Sharpton speaks directly to a larger and more vital issue: its role in consistently subverting honest racial discourse in this country. The media narrative is that racial intolerance remains pervasive in America—but only on one side of the political spectrum. This has not only justified media bias on behalf of affirmative action and other government programs designed to address persistent racism, but it has enabled leftist partisans, including more than a few journalists themselves, to confidently smear those with contrary views as bigots. Even on those rare occasions when race baiters on the left find themselves on the defensive, conservatives, so the narrative goes, are the true villains. Thus it was, for example, that during the height of the firestorm over Obama mentor Jeremiah Wright, *Wired* magazine's Spencer Ackerman proposed to his fellow leftists on JournoList that they distract public attention from Wright by destroying the reputations of key conservatives. "If the right forces us all to either defend Wright or tear him down, no matter what we choose, we lose the game they've put upon us," he wrote, in a message he never expected to see the light of day. "Instead, take one of them— Fred Barnes, Karl Rove, who cares—and call them racists." Though the revelation briefly provoked outrage on the right, it was largely ignored by the mainstream press and the impact on Ackerman's career was nonexistent.

Yet, heedless, the media continue to cast themselves as the nation's racial referees, ruling on what might and might not be appropriately said, and who might say it, and otherwise enforcing liberal orthodoxy.

Case in point: coverage of the Tea Party movement.

That the left should have sought to portray as driven by racism a movement built around limited government and economic freedom—a.k.a., the nation's founding principles—was pretty bizarre in the first place, but at least understandable, in the same way as the desert mole rat's tendency when cornered is to run blindly backward; it is genetically encoded. But that the media would so readily collude in such a baseless slur surprised even some of its harshest critics.

"Tainting the Tea Party movement with the charge of racism is proving to be an effective strategy for Democrats," said Mary Frances Berry, a leftist academic and former chairwoman of the U.S. Commission on Civil Rights, who was foolish enough to publicly enthuse of the media's reliably passing on of Democrat talking points as fact. "There is no evidence that Tea Party adherents are any more racist than other Republicans, and indeed many other Americans. But getting them to spend their time purging their ranks and having candidates distance themselves should help Democrats win in November. Having one's opponent rebut charges of racism is far better than discussing joblessness."

So unrelenting was the bigotry charge that the Tea Party stalwarts of FreedomWorks felt obliged to launch an effort called "DiverseTea," replete with minority outreach TV ads showcasing movement participants with darker complexions. The point, observed FreedomWorks head Matt Kibbe, was to counter "this nagging perception that we are not diverse." Talk about a fool's game! As one conservative blogger accurately noted, such an effort succeeded only in "enabling of far-left concepts," and was doomed from the outset. As George Wallace once vowed never to be "out-niggered again," so the left will never be out-diversified or out-multiculturaled.

The media's shamelessness was most blatantly on display on March 20, 2010, when several black Democratic congressmen, including Georgia's John Lewis, walked through a crowd of angry Tea Partiers protesting the imminent passage of Obama-Care outside the Capitol. Lewis's colleague, André Carson of Indiana (who a year later would say of Tea Party-supported congressional colleagues, they "would love to see you and me hanging on a tree") immediately approached a group of reporters claiming that the n-word had been shouted their way "at least 15 times." There exists a recording of this moment, and it shows the reporters uncritically accepting Carson's account at face value, as well as that of his colleague Emanuel Cleaver, who claimed he'd been spat at.

This incident, "evidence" of Tea Party bigotry, was an instant media sensation, with pundits everywhere denouncing the vile behavior of the right-wing zealots. There was particular focus on Congressman Lewis, who 45 years before, facing down an earlier generation of racists in Selma, Alabama, had been badly beaten by police.

"Tea party protesters call Georgia's John Lewis 'nigger'" ran the shocking headline over the story by the reporter for the McClatchy Newspapers chain, representing, among others, the *Miami Herald*, the *Kansas City Star*, and the *Sacramento Bee*. "Demonstrators outside the U.S. Capitol, angry over the proposed health care bill, shouted 'nigger' Saturday at U.S. Rep. John Lewis, a Georgia congressman and civil rights icon who was nearly beaten to death during an Alabama march in the 1960s," the article began.

"The protesters also shouted obscenities at other members of the Congressional Black Caucus, lawmakers said.

"'They were shouting, sort of harassing,' Lewis said. 'But, it's okay, I've faced this before. It reminded me of the sixties. It was a lot of downright hate and anger and people being down-right mean.'"

The tone they took of shock, horror, and disgust was the same in other outlets. "Past strife and jeers, another long march in the name of change," went the headline of the *New York Times's* piece, which went on to stirringly describe how Lewis "joined hands with fellow House Democrats and marched past jeering protesters into the Capitol to remake the nation's health care system. 'Today we are walking again, and we will be walking into history,' Mr. Lewis, a Georgian, said as the House neared the climax of a marathon health care debate that has stirred partisan passions across the nation and allowed Democrats to claim an achievement that has eluded them for decades. 'This is our time.'"

The *Washington Post's* coverage, meanwhile, featured a series of quotes from Lewis's Democratic colleagues. "'I have heard things today that I have not heard since March 15, 1960, when I was marching to get off the back of the bus,' said House Majority Whip James Clyburn (D-S.C.), the highest-ranking black official in Congress.

"And Majority Leader Steny H. Hoyer (D-Md.) said in a statement, 'On the one hand, I am saddened that America's debate on health care—which could have been a national con-versation of substance and respect—has degenerated to the point of such anger and incivility. But on the other, I know that every step toward a more just America has aroused similar hate in its own time; and I know that John Lewis, a hero of the civil rights movement, has learned to wear the worst slurs as a badge of honor.'"

Over on PBS, Tavis Smiley weighed in with the odd claim that Tea Partiers "every day . . . are being recently arrested for making threats against elected officials, for calling people 'nig-ger' as they walk into Capitol Hill, for spitting on people."

Then there was NBC, in the person of Andrea Mitchell. From the transcript:

Andrea Mitchell: They spat at Congressman Emanuel Cleaver, used the n-word against civil rights icon John Lewis, who was beaten and bloodied at the Selma March 45 years ago.

Representative James Clyburn (Democrat, South Carolina): They heard those words being used. And when you looked at some of the signs that were painted out there, putting a Hitler-like mustache on President Obama and other things that carried double meanings . . .

Mitchell: Some Republican members egged them on, waving signs from a balcony.

There was just one problem with all of this. The incident, at least as described and so widely disseminated, never happened. The protesters themselves denied it and, far more relevant, no one seems to have recorded the offending words—this despite the fact that innumerable cameras and recording devices were present. Within a week, conservative activist Andrew Breitbart was publicly calling Carson a liar, and offering $10,000 of his own money (to be donated to the United Negro College Fund) to anyone who could offer evidence otherwise.

No such evidence was ever forthcoming, and evidently no attempt to find any seemed to have been made—at least by mainstream outlets. That would have been called *journalism.*

Not that the absence of evidence altered the way media continued to report the story, not with the original version fitting so neatly into its overarching Tea Party equals racism narrative. Facts be damned, columnists and commentators continued to carry the highly distorted initial account well after it dropped off the front pages. At the *Times* alone, Frank Rich railed in one column about how "civil rights hero John Lewis has been slimed by these vigilantes," and in another about "watching goons hurl venomous slurs at congressmen like the civil rights hero John Lewis." His colleague Maureen Dowd weighed in with how Tea Partiers "outside the Capitol on Saturday called two black congressmen, the civil rights hero John Lewis of Georgia and André Carson of Indiana, a racial epithet as they walked by. Another, Representative Emanuel Cleaver of Missouri, was called that epithet and got spit on." And Bob Herbert wrote of how "opponents of the health care legislation spit on a black congressman and shouted racial slurs at two others, including John Lewis, one of the great heroes of the civil rights movement."

Indeed, a quick Nexis survey shows that in media reports John Lewis was linked to the term "civil rights hero" 84 times, and to "civil rights icon" 124 times. (Never mind that his long-ago bravery in Selma seems to be the only laudable entry in an otherwise mediocre record as a party hack; and that his 12 terms in Congress have in fact been marked by his failure to take even a meaningful single vote suggesting courage.)

Someone who will never be called a civil rights hero by Lewis's media fans—but surely also qualifies for the title—is Charles Pickering, the Mississippi federal district judge nominated by George W. Bush in 2001 to the U.S. Court of Appeals for the Fifth Circuit. The contrast is immensely revealing.

That liberals would fight Pickering's nomination is understandable, even a given. An unabashed conservative and strict constructionist, his history indicated he would take the opposite side from theirs on a range of contentious issues. In *A Price Too High*, the book he wrote on his confirmation battle, he mockingly refers to the liberals' "living Constitution" as the "mystery Constitution" and worries over the long-term consequences of an activist judiciary. Moreover, at the 1976 Republican National Convention, Pickering chaired a subcommittee that recommended the plank opposing *Roe v. Wade*.

Nonetheless, by every standard, Pickering's record on the bench was exemplary, and when he received the American Bar Association's highest rating of "well qualified," it appeared the nomination was likely to sail through the Senate.

But activists from left-liberal special-interest groups, led by Ralph Neas of People for the American Way, took charge of the opposition, and, aided by sympathetic journalists, they did a staggeringly ugly hit job on the courtly 64-year-old grandfather. Speaking of Nexis, a search for the terms "Pickering" and "racist" will yield more than 600 hits. Under ordinary circumstances, a false racism charge, made for obviously political reasons, is reprehensible. In Pickering's case, it was worse. For in civil rights-era Mississippi, when courage among whites was at a premium, he was among the handful who literally put his life at risk on behalf of equal rights. The fact is, were he on the other side of the political spectrum, liberals would rush to embrace him as a moral exemplar.

Years before, as a young lawyer, Pickering had settled his family in the central Mississippi town of Laurel. As it happened, Laurel was home to the White Knights of the KKK, under Imperial Wizard Sam Bowers, the most vicious of all Klan organizations. Described by *Time* as "the most dangerous man ever to wear a white hood," Bowers was behind innumerable acts of terror, including the infamous murders of civil rights workers Andrew Goodman, Michael Schwerner, and James Chaney.

"Blacks around here lived in mortal fear," recalled Melvin Mack, a black man who in recent times went on to be Laurel's mayor. "Around here, when the Klan marched in the streets, they didn't wear hoods, because they wanted us to know who they were."

"I remember when the Freedom Riders started coming to Laurel," added Pickering, when I reported on the case.

"It's almost impossible to describe it, the venom was so great. These thugs would take out their blackjacks and start brutally beating these young African Americans." In fact, as Mayor Mack remembers, they'd do it "smack in the middle of a black neighborhood, so he could rub it in our faces. They knew they wouldn't be prosecuted—and if they were, they weren't gonna be convicted."

But when Pickering was elected prosecuting attorney for Jones County in 1963, he took Bowers and the Klan on. "There'd been more than a hundred acts just locally—beatings, fire bombings, shooting into homes," as he told me, and in 1967, he finally succeeded in having Bowers arrested, charged with the murder of a local black activist. At the trial, Pickering took the stand against him. In spite of overwhelming evidence of Bowers's guilt, the jury was hung and he was released.

Asked today if he feared for his personal safety, Pickering concedes: "There was just one time that really gave me pause. I had prosecuted a Klansman who'd brutally beaten a local businessman, and a little while after that, I learned that the Klan had put out a 'No. two' on me—that was code for a beating. So for a while, I did take special care when I left my office at night. But, you know, when you're young, you really don't spend much time thinking about those things."

Mississippi's public schools integrated in 1969, which in many districts across the state resulted in white parents enrolling their children in newly created all-white academies. "That didn't happen in Laurel," recalled Pickering's son Chip, who entered first grade that year, "mainly because my father and a handful of other community leaders believed so strongly in public education." In the end, all four of the Pickering kids graduated from the local public high school, with Chip playing quarterback—"second string," points out his friend, Mayor Mack—on the largely black football team.

That unwavering commitment to a nation of laws and not of men had, Pickering asserted at the time of his nomination, also dictated his behavior on the bench. Indeed, he pointed out that in the past it had been judicial activism from the *right* that was most damaging to core American values, citing the infamous *Dred Scott* and *Plessy v. Ferguson* decisions. In an article for the Federalist Society, Pickering approvingly noted that Justice Benjamin R. Curtis quit the Supreme Court in the wake of the Dred Scott decision—the only person ever to do so as a matter of principle.

But all that was immaterial to his ideological foes who, picking through the nominee's voluminous records—supplied by the victim himself, in one of the crueler aspects of the process—pieced together an attack plan. Finding scant ammunition, they fell back on what, for elite liberals, was the obvious: as a white Mississippian during the Jim Crow era, Pickering was, by definition, morally backward. Unearthing several isolated episodes from Pickering's career, they presented them out of context, summoning up, as People for the American Way had it, a "troubling pattern" of "racial insensitivity." Marcia Kuntz of the Alliance for Justice went even further, declaring Pickering "a throwback to the old, segregated South."

Among the evidence cited to support these outlandish claims was a law-review note that Pickering wrote as a first-year law student in 1959, suggesting that the language of the Mississippi statute banning interracial marriage be altered if the law "is to serve the purpose that the Legislature undoubtedly intended it to serve"; his alleged sympathies as a state legislator for the pro-segregation Mississippi Sovereignty Commission; and, most damning of all, the charge that, in a 1994 case in his district courtroom, he'd shown leniency toward a convicted cross burner.

Initially, Pickering's Bush administration allies deemed these charges so weak as to scarcely take them seriously. In the nearly half-century-old law-school note, Pickering had been making a technical point, rather than commenting on the content of the law; in any case, even some liberals conceded that it was unreasonable to apply contemporary racial sensibilities to the Jim Crow South, especially since at the time overwhelming majorities of whites and blacks, in the North as well as the South, frowned on interracial marriage. On the Sovereignty Commission charge, as a Cox News Service reporter who investigated the matter observed, by the time Pickering voted as a state senator to fund the commission—in 1972 and 1973—"Mississippi had generally dismantled legal segregation, and the agency was trying to retool itself as a general investigative organization."

For shock value alone, the cross-burning charge appeared the most disturbing. But an even passing acquaintance with the specifics of the case proved it entirely baseless. Daniel Swan, the defendant in *United States v. Swan*, was a 20-year-old with no prior arrests or record of hostility to blacks who claimed to have been drunk when he and two others set a makeshift cross aflame in front of the home of an interracial couple. Evidence established that one of the two others was the ringleader—in fact, had earlier fired a shot into the couple's home—but he was 17, so was allowed to plead guilty without prison time; as was the third man, 25, on the grounds that he was mentally incompetent. Offered an 18-month sentence by Janet Reno's Justice Department, Swan instead chose to go to trial. Once convicted, he faced a possible seven and a half years. Pickering, who had a history of cutting breaks to young defendants with no priors, both black and white, gave him 27 months and a stern tongue-lashing. He had committed "a despicable act," said the judge. "The type of conduct you exhibited cannot and will not be tolerated." Pickering added, "During the time that you're in prison . . . do some reading on race relations and maintaining good race relations and how that can be done."

As the attacks against Pickering escalated, Mississippians of both parties and races rallied behind his candidacy, as did every paper in the state. In the Senate itself, Lindsey Graham of South Carolina assumed the role of surrogate for all those affronted Mississippians. Graham asked: "Do you know what it must have been like in 1967 to get on the stand and testify against the Ku Klux Klan in Mississippi? Do you have any idea what courage that took? Shame on you."

Meanwhile, reporters for a number of papers, including the *New York Times*, journeyed to Mississippi, heard the truth and told it in their stories. Nonetheless, activist liberal editorialists and commentators went after Pickering hammer and tongs. Most notably, in multiple editorials, the highly influential *New York Times* was unrelentingly brutal, and influential columnists Frank Rich and Maureen Dowd predictably followed suit; one writing of Pickering's "strenuous effort to reduce the sentence of a convicted cross-burning hoodlum" and the other of his "soft spot for cross-burners." "The *New York Times*' columnists and editorial writers either didn't read what their own reporters had written, or else they didn't care," Pickering put it to me later.

The most meaningful media defense of Pickering came from *60 Minutes* in March 2004. Pickering said he was initially uncertain about whether to cooperate with the show. "When you're Southern and conservative and the national news media comes down, you cringe a little bit," he said, "and Mike Wallace did have a reputation." But Wallace and his producer relished the chance to tell what, in their circles, was the man-bites-dog story of a Southern conservative unjustly accused of racism.

The star of the piece, aside from Pickering himself, was Charles Evers, brother of the martyred Medgar and a longtime civil rights champion in his own right who was one of several black defenders of the judge to make an appearance on the broadcast. After he'd finished his own interview before the camera, Evers asked if he could sit in on the next one, with Clarence McGee of the NAACP, one of the groups that had fought Pickering from the start. The result made for a riveting confrontation—and one that left the anti-Pickering forces revealed for what they were before a nationwide audience.

"You know that Charles Pickering was the man that helped us break the Ku Klux Klan?" challenged Evers, after McGee presented the NAACP's case. "Did you know that?" In response, McGee stammered that, no, he hadn't known that.

Evers: Well, I know that. Do you know about the young black man that was accused of robbing the young white woman? Do you know about that?

McGee: No.

Evers: So Charles Pickering took the case, came to trial, and won the case, and the young man became free.

McGee: I don't know about that.

Evers: All right. But did you also know that Charles Pickering is the man who helped integrate his—his churches? Do you know about that?

McGee: No.

Evers: Well, you don't know a thing about Charles Pickering.

"That young punk didn't know nothin' about nothing," Evers later recalled of the encounter. "That's all you gotta say in this country, a white man's a racist, this white man hates black folks. Well, I could not let them destroy a white man just because he's white, when I know different."

But, in fact, his opponents and their media allies did succeed in destroying Pickering, or at least his nomination. After four years in limbo, it was finally scuttled.

That, of course, has long been the impetus behind the racism charge, and for ideologically driven liberals, the ultimate justification: It worked, driving terror into hearts of all but the foolhardy few and silencing the rest.

But there are hopeful signs that that may at last be changing. With people all over the country flat-out sick of being smeared, an increasing number are no longer keeping quite so quiet about it. "I can't count the number of readers who have expressed to me the frustration they feel when they are branded bigots for expressing their concerns over subjects such as the Plaza mobs, President Barack Obama's policies, or Arizona's new immigration law," opined *Kansas City Star* ombudsman Derek Donovan in May 2010, speaking for public editors everywhere. "I agree that accusations of bigotry are a cheap tactic sometimes employed simply to shut down debate. It's a little like the classic gotcha: 'When did you stop beating your wife?' The stink of the accusation lingers, even if it's later shown to be without merit."

It has long been apparent that not only do the media tend to smear those who aggressively challenge the liberal line on race, but they routinely ignore *news* that casts doubt on that line. For instance, in major news organizations' ongoing coverage of what they take to be the sin of racial profiling, it is almost never pointed out that the tactic is effective precisely because an inordinate percentage of criminals in those areas are black; or that its main beneficiaries are themselves black. Indeed, sometimes their ability to avoid key facts borders on the laughable. Back in late December 2010, to light on one particularly striking instance, the New York tabloids ran screaming headlines about the extraordinary reaction of Fernando Mateo, a leader of the New York Federation of Taxi Drivers, to the shooting the night before of one of his cabbies, a black man named Trevor Bell. "You know, sometimes it's good we are racially profiled," said the infuriated Mateo, himself black and Hispanic. "Because the God's honest truth is 99 percent of the people that are robbing, stealing, killing these drivers are black and Hispanics."

The *New York Times* could not avoid covering the shooting of Trevor Bell, and its reporter also quoted Mateo. In the *Times* story, Mateo said that Bell began driving a livery cab after being laid off from a construction job, and noted he was working that night only because he was "trying to put his pennies together for the Christmas holiday." But there was not a single word reporting the *real* news: the union leader's brave and heretical views on racial profiling.

Then, again, this is the way it tends to go with issues of every kind that involve a strong racial element. Take the effort by congressional Republicans to defund Head Start, the well-intentioned program aimed at giving lower income nursery school-aged kids an educational leg up to help them succeed in later grades. In place since the sixties, the program is a favorite of liberals, and the mainstream media naturally lined up against what was described as an especially draconian cut. What they failed to report was that, in fact, Head Start was a failure; it has never produced the hoped-for results. Moreover, a study of 4,600 preschoolers by the U.S. Department of Health and Human Resources made that sad failure clear beyond all question. Yet, as columnist Mona Charen noted, the study got almost no coverage. "Hardly a whimper. A few conservative websites like Heritage, CATO, and the Independent Women's

Forum noted the results, but elsewhere, all was silence. Or, not silence actually, complete denial. President Obama had boosted funding for Head Start from $6.8 billion in 2008 to $9.2 billion in 2009. Secretary of Health and Human Services Kathleen Sebelius and Education Secretary Arne Duncan support even greater 'investments' in the failed program in the future. Study? What study?"

Victor Davis Hanson, a fellow at the conservative Hoover Institution at Stanford University, in September 2010 blogged on another verboten topic: American universities' diversity obsession, observing that "the university is the most politically intolerant and monolithic institution in the country, even as it demands the continuance of tenure to protect supposedly unpopular expression. Even its emphases on racial diversity is entirely constructed and absurd: Latin Americans add an accent and a trill and they become victimized Chicanos; one-half African Americans claim they are more people of color than much darker Punjabis; the children of Asian optometrists seek minority and victim status."

In response, the aspiring *New York Times* journalists at the school's paper, the *Stanford Daily*, issued a blistering editorial attack on Hanson, calling his observations "absolute trash" and "at best vitriolic ignorance," and urging that the university "repudiate or, at the very least, review Hanson's remarks. Surely, gross generalities couched in racially charged language cannot fit with Hoover's mission. . . . Thus, we issue this editorial as an open challenge to the Hoover Institution."

It was the sort of broadside that even now would have most academics quaking in their loafers, bringing forth a slavish apology or, at the very least, a mealy mouthed public statement heavy with terms like "out of context" and "misunderstood." But, no, what Hanson did instead was counterattack, and with the sort of fearless bravado he's so often written about in his distinguished career as a military historian. Branding the editorial with a term certain to put liberals on the defensive—"McCarthyite"—he pointed out that his "examples were not cheap, toxic, or despicable, but drawn from my own experience with higher education over some 40 years as both student and professor, in which tragically the university often discriminated against students of all races and heritages by applying fossilized racial categories that have no place in 21st-century America." He then leveled "an open challenge to the *Stanford Daily*: Either apologize for the baseless slur of racism and the cheap language (e.g., "trash," "toxic," "despicable"), or at least show how I was in error, and that, in fact, there are logical and consistent criteria that qualify some groups for racial preference in admissions and hiring in the university and not others." The longtime reflex, he concluded, has been "to call critics racists rather than to present a logical and consistent defense of the so often illogical and inconsistent. That simply will not work anymore."

Instantly, Hanson's broadside was picked up by a slew of sympathetic websites, notably the hugely popular Instapundit, and in short order the muddle-headed name callers at the *Daily* were swamped by letters from aroused citizens throughout the land. "Brown Shirts . . . all of you," charged one typical missive. "If people had to buy the ideas you have to sell, you'd be dirt poor," read another. "That kind of knee jerk demonization of anyone who questions race-conscious resource allocation by powerful institutions is daily becoming less and less convincing," offered a third. "Time to stop playing the race card and start making real arguments."

Is it too much to hope that the sophomores and juniors poring over these missives might take a break from their smirking to take seriously what they say and reflect on concepts like fairness and professional responsibility? Probably. But at least they're learning that the noxious charge of racism is no longer sure to go unchallenged.

Of course, it is too late for the smug veterans of the sixties setting the racial agenda at key mainstream outlets. Until they and/or their publications retire to the big commune in the sky, we'll continue to endure their coverage of an imaginary world where every black person is a potential victim, and every charge of racism, no matter how scurrilous, is presumed credible.

Look no further than 2006's notorious Duke lacrosse rape case. Here you had clear signs from the very start that a black stripper's accusation that she had been gang raped by a group of white Duke jocks was, at the least, highly suspect. There was no corroborating physical evidence of rape or sodomy and firm proof that at least one of the accused was elsewhere at the time of the alleged assault. Meanwhile, Michael Nifong, the highly ambitious, up-for-election prosecutor driving the case, seemed disinclined to even consider the possibility the accused lacrosse players might be innocent, never mind that the accuser was unstable and her story seemed to change daily. Ultimately, of course, the case collapsed, and the odious Nifong, having kept key evidence from defense lawyers, was disbarred and made to serve a symbolic one-day jail sentence.

Still, incredibly, the media kept up the drumbeat against the accused even as the case fell apart, every bit as eager as the hardcore leftists on the Duke faculty to see their irresistible tale—a single black working mother in the Deep South savaged by latter-day plantation owners' sons—confirmed by a conviction.

Needless to say, by April 2011, when the Duke accuser, Crystal Mangum, briefly resurfaced in the news—indicted in the stabbing death of her boyfriend—the disgraced role played by the media in the Duke case had long since disappeared down the journalistic memory hole.

The worst offender? You guessed it. The *New York Times* took particular pleasure in spinning out the satisfying narrative: running innumerable damning pieces about the accused lacrosse players, decrying the sports culture that supposedly created them, and otherwise endlessly indulging their taste for black and female victimhood. It displayed an almost painful reluctance to give it up even as the story was unraveling. The one *Times* reporter who publicly expressed any doubts about its veracity was taken off the beat, replaced by a compliant ideological hack. Indeed, while other outlets were starting to run in the other direction, the *Times* produced a front-page defense of Nifong's determination to press the prosecution.

In early 2011, HBO announced it had acquired the rights to an excellent book on the Duke case, K.C. Johnson and Stuart Taylor Jr.'s *Until Proven Innocent: Political Correctness and the Shameful Injustices of the Duke Lacrosse Rape Case*. There is, of course, a rich history of great movies about Southern racial injustice—from *The Defiant Ones* and *In the Heat of the Night*, to *To Kill a Mockingbird* and *Ghosts of Mississippi*—and this story certainly has all the elements for another: a vicious, false accusation, pushed by an ambitious prosecutor and the local establishment; heroic defendants and their tireless defense team standing firm against all odds for the truth; a cadre of villainous outsiders (i.e., the *New York Times*, et al.).

HBO being what it is—a determinedly liberal operation—the appropriate reaction to such a development must be caution. The likelihood is that, assuming the film actually gets made, it will be larded with paeans to multiculturalism, diversity, and all the rest. Still, there's no way the Timesmen can possibly be transformed into good guys, or the racism accusation into anything but the vicious slur it was. And in the media universe as we find it, that alone counts as progress.

LET'S PRETEND NO. 1
AFFIRMATIVE ACTION IS REASONABLE, NOT RACIST

Affirmative action is a nightmare.

Indeed, racial preferences—the less weasely term for the thing—might as well have been designed to mock everything that America stands for in principle. From the 18th-century aphorisms of Ben Franklin to the moral lessons of Horatio Alger a hundred years later, to the sorts of advice offered by business best sellers and iconic sports coaches today, Americans have always embraced the notion that our country is an aristocracy of merit, a place where, regardless of background or social standing, anything is possible if one has the talent and works hard enough. And even to the extent we sometimes fall short of this animating ideal, it is one we cling to, and seek to pass on to our kids. For the more than two and a quarter centuries of our existence as a nation, it is this uniquely American sense of possibility that has impelled people from all parts of the world to leave behind their old lives and come here; if not for their own sake, for their children's.

I think back on my Uncle Sol. He was four years old in the first decade of the 20th century when he arrived with my grandparents on these shores from what is now Poland. A dozen years later, through dogged effort, he succeeded in winning a full scholarship to New York University and went on to graduate first in his class with a degree in chemical engineering. But this was the mid-1920s, and at the time major chemical companies, like DuPont, were not hiring Jews; in two years of trying, Sol failed to land a job in his chosen field. So he returned to school and became a pharmacist instead. Yet odd as it may strike the modern sensibility, he was never bitter. For all his loathing of discrimination, he never stopped believing in America and its promise, and lived long enough to see the inequities he most detested—the quotas that barred so many Jews from certain industries and elite universities—disappear.

As it happens, Sol died shortly before affirmative action became standard practice in American higher education and the business world, which is fortunate. For the notion that today people like him would *again* be discriminated against—only this time for being white and male—might have killed him all over again.

Of course, that is not how most black people (and to a lesser extent, Hispanics) see it. According to a typical poll, released by Quinnipiac in 2009, when asked "Do you think affirmative action programs that give preferences to blacks and other minorities in hiring, promotions and college admissions should be continued, or do you think these affirmative action programs should be abolished?" whites favored "abolished" 64–27, while blacks favored "continued" by a staggering 78–14.

Given that so many blacks buy into the notion that, even today, it is primarily racism that is keeping them down, this is understandable. After all, if things really were so stacked against them, there would be no possible way for them to succeed in meaningful numbers in today's America without the benefit of what in any other universe would be regarded as an unfair advantage. And if such a remedy means that blameless others get screwed in the process, so be it.

Or, wait, maybe that's just a mean-spirited, conservative characterization of an enlightened system that seeks only to put everyone on an equal footing. Having found myself in innumerable heated exchanges over the years with affirmative action proponents, most of them white liberals, I have no doubt most truly believe racial preferences are about fairness. And justice. And, indeed, far from turning our backs on what we profess to believe, living up to it.

Then, again, more than once, after the affirmative action supporter's gotten a few drinks in him, I've also heard about score settling. Sure, preferences are discriminatory, one liberal family member acknowledged at a family gathering a few years back, but so what! Black people suffered for centuries, while we whites reaped every imaginable benefit. So—this is verbatim—"Tough, now it's their turn."

In jousting with such people, I like to bring up their own children, and wonder how they'd feel if it were *they* losing out on a place at college or a good job to a less qualified minority. Alas, in the case of this woman, the question actually elicited a new burst of self-satisfaction. "Something like that probably did happen when my son got turned down at Yale," she said. "I told him that it was a necessary sacrifice—and he understood." What's worse, I'm not even sure she was lying.

However such conversations with white liberals begin, and no matter where they go, somewhere along the way they always end up touching on the "legacy of slavery," and the ways "the old boys network" has long privileged whites, and how while things may be getting better, "we're not there yet."

This has been the line for quite a while now. Affirmative action got seriously going under President Lyndon B. Johnson, and we can argue forever about how necessary it was even then; certainly, a far more compelling case could have been made. But what's beyond question is that the returns have been diminishing for a long time now, and that at this point the vast preferences machine endlessly churns into the American mainstream a toxic mix of bitterness and misunderstanding between the races.

I was exposed to an extended dose of it back in the spring of 2008, when my wife and I spent some time in St. Louis gathering signatures for a proposed initiative aimed at getting an anti-affirmative action measure on the Missouri state ballot. We soon figured out that among the most likely places to find eager signers was in the parking lots outside Lowes or Home Depot superstores. We'd get there early, around 7:30 a.m., because that's when contractors would begin showing up in their pickups or vans. My come-on was brief and to the point— "Sign my petition to end affirmative action?"—and it was generally greeted with some version of either: a resigned "That'll never happen, not in this lifetime"; or an eager "How many times can I sign?" Often, those replies came with harangues about the government and its misbegotten policies—a particular sore spot was the "minority set aside" that left them ineligible for work on a new stadium being built across the state in Kansas City—and sometimes, too, there were stories. Several guys told me they'd had to hire blacks to front their businesses, so as to nab contracts for which they'd otherwise not have been considered; one had made the elderly black woman who cared for his mother "president" of his firm. Another guy reported he had a black friend who'd managed to get himself named to the boards of several construction firms, each of which paid him a stipend for doing nothing at all.

Almost to a man, and they were *all* men, the early arrivals were white. We rarely saw a black guy until after nine, which is usually just before an officious employee would emerge from the store and inform us there'd been a complaint and we'd better depart the property or they'd have to call the cops. The same thing happened at one of my other most productive signature gathering spots, outside a White Castle during lunch hour. Clipboard in hand, I simply stood by the drive leading to the take-out window and made my pitch to drivers as they pulled alongside. In 10 minutes I got more than 30 signatures by this method, before a car pulled up with a black woman behind the wheel. "Sign my petition to end affirmative action?" I asked, smiling.

"No!" she coldly shot back, the voice of doom. I managed to get only a couple of more signatures before she reached the window.

Truth be told, I generally avoided asking black people to sign, even when doing so wouldn't have meant instant eviction. There was simply no percentage in it, either practically or emotionally. The chances of bagging a signature were slight, and those of being regarded with loathing were pretty high. Had I been interested in getting into arguments about how I was *not* a racist, there were less uncomfortable people to have it with, starting with the smug NPR types we were continually running across.

But once in a while such a request was unavoidable—and in every such case, I got my signature, which made these episodes especially instructive. For each time I asked a black person to sign my petition, it was when he was among white people, so seemingly feeling pressure not to be the odd man out. These moments were usually a matter of happenstance. One day, for instance, I went into a place in a strip mall that produced and sold trophies and made my pitch to the guy behind the counter. He was so delighted at the prospect of seeing such a measure on the ballot that after signing, he led me out back, where the things were manufactured, so I could gather more. There were eight or 10 guys working the molds and presses, and one by one he took me to their work stations. All signed enthusiastically, one even requesting blank petitions so he could pass them around to friends. The black guy, middle aged with heavy horn-rimmed glasses, was at one of the louder machines, which he turned off; and after a long moment, he gave me his signature, but wordlessly and clearly without enthusiasm. Even as I thanked him, I felt a sharp twinge of sympathy for the guy, not just because I'd put him in this position, but because for him there so obviously was no right answer. Clearly a key part of the tight-knit trophy factory family, definitely not a beneficiary of racial preferences himself, perhaps even in general agreement with his co-workers on the issue, he nonetheless left me keenly feeling that his signature constituted for him an act of betrayal.

In this sense, and there are others, this corrosive, misbegotten system is also a terrible deal for black people. The look on the face of that guy in the trophy place bespoke an anguish every bit as real as that of the white guys getting screwed out of work because of the color of their skin. They know full well how affirmative action affects the ways they are viewed by their fellow citizens; and, too, inevitably, conveying as it does the unmistakable message that they're so fundamentally handicapped they can't make it on their own, in innumerable cases it distorts how they see themselves.

Excellence is always a matter of pride and self-belief, the very qualities racial preferences undermine by definition. If there is no need to out-hustle one's competitors, and no expectation that one will, why even try? Perpetually focused on past inequities rather than future possibilities, the victim mindset epitomized by affirmative action not only saps energy and initiative, it *justifies* the absence of energy and initiative.

Not, to be sure, that very many of the minority contractors I encountered on the receiving end of the racial spoils system would willingly surrender the tremendous edge over white competitors handed them by their government. Versed in the rhetoric of victimization, encouraged in that attitude by guilty whites, "civil rights activists," and a popular culture that dwells endlessly on the bad old days, many feel legitimately entitled. Besides, as Democrats know—and count on every election season—no one likes his particular something-for-nothing taken away.

Yet no matter how readily they may justify that advantage based on their forebears' tragic history or even slights they've suffered personally, most surely grasp on some level that they're gaming the system. Nor does it take a doctorate in human behavioral science to know that such an assumption becomes internalized and self-fulfilling.

When I was discussing affirmative action not long ago with a liberal acquaintance, he brought up baseball, asserting "a black player has to be twice as good as a white guy to get the same job." This is one of those liberal truisms that was once inarguably true—and never more so than in the case of Jackie Robinson, which is part of what made his performance and that of the other black baseball pioneers so heroic. But it is simply no longer so, as a quick review of current major league rosters will show; not even in the case of marginal "bench" players, once useful as the centerpiece of such a claim. To the contrary, it is far more accurate to observe that in many realms of American life today (if not in sports), the black guy need be only half as good.

In fact, the elaborate system of pretense and outright falsehood at the heart of racial preferences must *inevitably* lead to inefficiency and corruption. As Heather Mac Donald points out in a piece on preferences in the construction industry, aptly titled "The Set-Aside Boondoggle," the rarely acknowledged reality is that "the real problem underlying minority under representation in the construction business" is not bias, but "inadequate skills." Indeed, she adds, "Government set-aside programs actually require inefficiency in infrastructure projects by demanding that the least competitive contractors be hired to work on them." Among her other deeply politically incorrect but on-target observations: Such programs "virtually force companies into deception, since there are not enough competent minority-owned companies to fill the quotas"; and "when 'disadvantaged' companies do actually participate on a project, rather than just acting as fronts, their suboptimal skills can require the hiring of additional workers to oversee or redo the quota employees' contribution."

The "suboptimal skills" of minorities of course bears perhaps even more directly on the controversy over affirmative action in college admissions. By now almost every junior and senior in every high school with a large college-bound student population is keenly aware of the advantages conferred upon those with the right skin pigmentation, or, for that matter, a lucky family history. In my kids' school, the father of one upper-middle-class fellow student happened to have been born and lived several years in Argentina, a stop in the family's postwar journey between Europe and America, which, never mind that he didn't speak a word of Spanish, enabled college admissions bean counters to slot him into the Hispanic category. Since he was a decent student, the kid was courted by several of the Ivies, while friends with comparable GPAs held zero interest for those same schools. Then there was the day my son and his friends were anxiously discussing their college prospects over lunch, when the black kid in the group nonchalantly observed, "Oh, I'll get in everywhere, because I'm black." And, of course, he was right.

"The new options have forced colleges to confront thorny questions, including how to account for various racial mixes in seeking diversity," reported the *New York Times*, in an approving June 2011 front-page piece on applicants of mixed race. "Is a student applying as black and Latino more desirable in terms of diversity than someone who is white and black? Or white and Vietnamese? Should the ethnicities of one's distant relatives be considered fair game, or just parents? And what should be done about students who skip the race question altogether—a sizable number of whom, some studies have shown, are white, and do so either in protest or out of fear that identifying as merely white could hurt rather than help their chances in this new environment?"

The *Times* piece prompted my friend Roger Kimball, terming affirmative action "that great jewel of Orwellian Newspeak," to speculate in print that perhaps when it comes time for his white, middle-class son to apply to college, "he can argue, with all the authority of the latest PoMo theorists, that since race, like sex and nationality, is just a social construction, he is really a female black Indian from Nigeria? Maybe it's worth a try."

Kimball's piece elicited many spirited online responses, but one was especially winning. "When I was in high school, one of the most amazing things happened," wrote the reader, identifying himself as Zombie, and it is worth reproducing in full. "Our school had a Black Student Club which, as you might imagine, was populated entirely by black students. (Not all the black students, obviously—my school was 40 percent black at the time—the club was mostly joined by those black students who wanted to get into good colleges and beef up their resumes.) Well, word went around one day early in 12th grade that there was some sort of scholarship being made available for members of the Black Student Club who had above a certain grade point average. Sounded like a sweet deal.

"So, two smart-aleck white boys—not brainiacs, not jocks, not racists, just two sarcastic class clowns who thought it would be funny to see if they could get some of that scholarship cash—went down to the sign-up meeting for the Black Students Club and tried to join.

"Well, you can imagine the fracas that broke out. The teacher who sponsored the club (a black social studies teacher who wore a dashiki and an Africa-shaped pendant) told the boys they couldn't join and tried to kick them out of the room. The smart-alecks were not intimidated—they asked 'Why can't we join?' And the response was emphatic: 'Because you're not black!'

"And then the boys did something amazing. They said, 'Yes, we are!' The teacher thundered, 'No, you're not!' And so the boys threw down the gauntlet: 'PROVE IT! Prove we're not black! Otherwise, you have to let us in.'

"Wow! Suddenly, the school was in a hell of a pickle. In order to keep the white-looking boys out of the club, the district would have to conduct some sort of racial purity trial to prove, legally, that the boys did not possess sufficient amounts of the desirable African-American blood. It would have been something straight out of the Nazi era or the Jim Crow south. A trial to prove someone was of a certain race so that they could be discriminated against!

"After several tense days, the school district decided that this was a lose-lose scenario for them, and that a trial would have been a public relations disaster of epic proportions. So they ordered the black teacher-sponsor to admit the white students to the Black Students Club.

"The teacher was outraged, but had no choice. He let them in. The two boys then became sort of playground heroes for smashing the race-based policies of the asshole adults.

"But the story has a not-so-happy ending. Shortly thereafter, the Black Students Club met en masse and voted to disband the club entirely, for the specific reason of not letting the white boys remain as members. And then later, when the hubbub died down, they formed a 'new' club called the African-American Students Club, with all the same members—except the two white boys.

"This time, they didn't bother repeating their stunt. Their point had been made.

"I think that if this concept was repeated across the country, all race-based policies would crumble."

Would that it were so.

In fact, part of the rarely mentioned collateral damage of affirmative action is that it turns the idealistic young into hardened cynics.

For when it comes to race and college admissions, cynicism is not just the name of the game, but its very essence. It has been at least since 1978, when the Supreme Court's *Regents of the University of California v. Bakke* decision introduced millions of unsuspecting Americans to the way racial preferences operate in our finest institutions of higher learning. Twice turned down for admission to the medical school at the University of California, Davis despite having better grades and test scores than most accepted minorities, Allan Bakke was deemed by the court a victim of reverse discrimination and allowed to enter the school. But, in a decision of stupefying illogic, the justices upheld affirmative action in *principle*, enabling colleges to make it a *consideration* in judging admissions applications. The result has been decades of schemes designed to enable administrators to continue to discriminate solely on the basis of race and ethnicity while pretending it is only one of many pertinent factors.

As it happened, the Bakke case had a tragic, but quite meaningful, addendum. In 1995, the *New York Times Magazine* ran a 10-page piece (by Nicholas Lemann, now dean of the Columbia School of Journalism) about Dr. Patrick Chavis, one of the black students admitted to Davis's med school over Allen Bakke, revealing that upon graduating Chavis had returned to the Los Angeles inner-city Compton neighborhood where he'd grown up and was serving its minority population as an obstetrician and gynecologist. As if the message wasn't sufficiently clear, the piece had Ted Kennedy lauding Chavis as a "perfect example" of the need for preferences. As an editorial in the *St. Louis Post Dispatch* snarkily observed, "Allan Bakke, admitted to medical school as a result of the lawsuit, is an anesthesiologist in Rochester, Minn. Patrick Chavis—the black son of a welfare mother who had been admitted with lower scores than Mr. Bakke—is a gynecologist serving poor Medicaid mothers in southern California. The social advantages of diversity continue to reverberate after graduation." To the *New York Times*, a typical preferences enthusiast wrote: "If this means educating people with lower grade-point averages but greater commitment to helping people who need it, so be it. Manhattan and Boca Raton can make do with a few less corporate merger attorneys and cosmetic surgeons."

Except the real lesson Patrick Chavis's story imparted in the end was altogether different. Just two years later, in 1998, the Medical Board of California revoked his license for "gross negligence, incompetence and repeated negligent acts" based on more than 90 misconduct charges, including the mistreatment of eight liposuction patients, one of whom died. In fact, it turned out that even before the appearance of the glowing

Times profile, he'd been sued for malpractice multiple times, and as far back as 1993, one Los Angeles hospital had been closely monitoring him after a botched delivery—for which he'd sued the hospital, charging racism.

It only got worse. In 2002, four years after losing his license, Chavis was killed in what police said was a failed hijacking attempt in inner-city L.A.

More than just a tragedy, the story was widely—and rightly—taken as a cautionary tale about affirmative action, driving home with special potency the reality that merit matters and, especially in life-and-death endeavors, cutting people a break based on race is a prescription for disaster.

But, of course, this is simple common sense—which is why so many of us not only regard minority doctors who benefited from affirmative action with skepticism, but tend, just in case, to be dubious about almost *any* minority doctor whose pedigree is unknown. This cuts a broad swath across ideological lines. Show me a liberal who says he's entirely comfortable being wheeled in for a heart bypass with a surgeon who got where he is via affirmative action—or getting into an airplane flown by an affirmative action pilot, or putting his life savings in the hands of an affirmative action money manager—and I'll show you a liar or a fool. True, the vast majority of those people might be fully competent, but why take the risk? Too many are where they are, not by virtue of prior achievement or demonstrable merit, but because of their ethnicity.

The doubts about the ability of blacks to do vital jobs as well as others are unquestionably the ugliest consequence of the preferences regime. In most cases, those questions are surely unfair and demeaning, but as long as decisions on college acceptance and hiring are made on any basis but merit, they will remain a harsh fact of American life. "When I was in the Air Force I was an instructor at a technical training facility where we were training officers," as some guy typically writes on an Internet forum, one of literally thousands that could be cited. "I was tasked to attempt to determine if there was a minimum qualification test entry score that would help weed out poorly qualified students. . . . When the data were looked at more closely based on race, the study was discarded because almost all students with low scores were minorities. Some of these folks could not write a complete sentence or compute the speed of an airplane given the numbers of miles covered in a minute even though they were all graduates from an accredited university."

Who knows, the guy who wrote that may be a total fraud, or a bigot just sticking in his vicious two cents. But, depressing as it is, it registers as credible precisely because it correlates with the experience of so many.

The very liberal Larry David had it just about right in an episode of *Curb Your Enthusiasm* titled "Affirmative Action." When Larry and his buddy Richard Lewis run into a black acquaintance of Richard, Larry asks who he is. "He's my dermatologist," Richard replies. "Really?" exclaims the ever-gauche Larry in obvious surprise, never mind that the guy is standing there.

Richard: For 15 years now.
Larry: Even with the whole affirmative-action thing?

The doctor is deeply offended, and so is an entire Beverly Hills roomful of his successful black professional friends when the story is repeated to them later in the episode, and why wouldn't they be?

But of course, we only laugh, uncomfortably, because it's true. The doctors and lawyers and entertainment execs in that room bear the stigma of affirmative action as surely as the least qualified inner-city kid struggling to keep up at a top-flight university. For the ultimate impact of racial preferences has been to place in question *all* black achievement.

Occasionally, *very* occasionally, even someone in the civil rights establishment acknowledges that painful truth. When, in March 2011, Eric Holder's Justice Department decreed that the Dayton, Ohio, Police Department alter its testing standards for recruits because too few African Americans had passed the exam—lowering the passing grade to 58 percent on part one of the exam and 63 percent on part two; i.e., to an F and a D, respectively—the head of the local branch of the NAACP joined Dayton's police union head in decrying the move as a threat to public safety. "The NAACP does not support individuals failing a test and then having the opportunity to be gainfully employed," said Dayton NAACP President Derrick Forward, on local TV. "If you lower the score for any group of people, you're not getting the best qualified people for the job."

Little wonder that no government-mandated policy has so firmly lodged itself in the nation's craw, or provoked such sustained opposition. The challenges to affirmative action have been incessant, often featuring individuals who, had they been on the other side of the issue, Hollywood would have rushed to embrace as avidly as they did environmental heroine Erin Brockovich or Jeffrey Wigand, the guy played by Russell Crowe who blew the whistle on the tobacco companies. Among the highest profile:

- Ward Connerly, who in 1996, took on California's powerful liberal and educational establishments to lead the fight for passage of state Proposition 209, amending the state constitution to ban the use of race, sex, or ethnicity in state hiring or university admissions.

As a University of California regent, Connerly had witnessed the corruption of the system first-hand, and during the campaign he effectively exposed it to the light of day. Needless to say, as a black man he faced ceaseless personal abuse as a "race traitor." During the Prop. 209 campaign, there seemed no filthy trick to which the measure's foes would not resort, including inviting KKK leader David Duke to the state as a "supporter" of the measure. None of it worked. Though massively outspent, the California Civil Rights Initiative campaign prevailed with 54 percent of the vote. Soon afterward, Connerly formed the American Civil Rights Institute, which in the years since has led similar campaigns in five other states.

• Jennifer Gratz was a Michigan high school student when she filed the lawsuit that eventually resulted in the landmark Supreme Court decision *Gratz v. Bollinger*. The daughter of a cop, Gratz was among the top students in her blue-collar suburban Detroit high school class with a 3.8 GPA, as well as a gifted athlete and the student council vice president, so as a graduating senior she was startled to be turned down by the University of Michigan's flagship Ann Arbor campus while minority friends of hers who were lesser students were accepted. It was later revealed that U-M ran a parallel admissions system for minorities, requiring markedly lower grades and test scores. Though the Supreme Court ultimately ruled in Gratz's favor, declaring that system illegal, it decreed it legitimate that institutions of higher learning seek "diversity" in their student body, enabling them to essentially continue to discriminate on the basis of race. Subsequently, working with Connerly, she spearheaded a 2006 ballot measure in Michigan that banned race-based admissions and hiring practices. Gratz left the ACRI in late 2011, charging her former colleague Connerly with financial irregularities. Their public falling out was a sad and shocking develop-ment, but (for all the pleasure it gave preferences supporters) no reflection on the remarkable work they did together.

- A New Haven, Connecticut, firefighter, Frank Ricci was one of 19 city firefighters—17 of them white, the other two Hispanic—who sued the city after they'd passed a rigorous exam for promotion, then seen the tests ruled invalid because no black firefighters had scored high enough to qualify. Ricci was an especially compelling and sympathetic figure since not only had he already amply demonstrated his leadership skills on the front lines in a field where competence matters more than just about any other, but he is dyslexic, so he had to study with special intensity to prep for the exam, and spent more than $1,000 to have books read onto audiotapes. Like Gratz, Ricci and his confeder-ates prevailed in the Supreme Court (though, again, by just a 5–4 margin), but the ruling scarcely gave pause to government diversicrats, who continue to devise set-aside programs in localities across the country.

Never mind the moral content of such programs; they are *economic* lunacy. In Tucson, Arizona, for example, women and minorities are given a 7 percent preference. Their bids are accepted on an equal basis with those of competitors that come in 7 percent lower.

Preference dead-enders will tell you they don't care about any of it, not the patent unfairness of the system, or the economic consequences, or even the powerful sense of injustice and ill usage it sows. There's nothing to be done about such people. In an obscene twist on Martin Luther King, they judge others *exclusively* by the color of their skin, and the hell with character. They are what they almost never get called—racists—and they will fight for their perverted version of justice till the bitter end.

Alas, the bitter end is not quite yet. Proponents of racial preferences are indefatigable, arguing their case with the passion of the possessed, endlessly mining statistical data to make the case that curbing preferences will cause irreparable harm. In the years following the passage of California's Proposition 209, for example, they pointed with horror to the precipitous drop in the acceptance of minorities to Berkeley and UCLA, the system's elite UC campuses. And, true enough, the decline was dramatic, fully 52 percent at Berkeley in 1998, the first year the anti-preferences measure took effect.

But if such statistics don't quite lie, neither do they tell the whole truth. For one thing, the primary beneficiaries of the end of affirmative action in California were not white students, whose numbers also dropped (from 40 percent in 1997 to 34 percent in 2005), but Asians; who having hitherto been classified, in the Orwellian bureaucratese so typical of such enterprises, as an "overrepresented minority"—we're talking, among others, the children of Vietnamese boat people—now flooded into the state universities in numbers appropriate to their academic achievement, by 2010 constituting fully 45.7 percent of incoming Berkeley freshmen.

But what the diversity zealots never get around to mentioning is that there has been a sharp *increase* in the number that actually corresponds to life success: the minority *graduation* rate. True enough, more were now attending the California system's less demanding state and community colleges, rather than its top universities, but they were flourishing. Whereas in the past, unprepared for the work at the elite campuses, they dropped out at alarming rates. Meanwhile, those who *were* admitted to the crown jewels of the California system, on the merits, today achieve graduation rates comparable to those of their white and Asian peers—at Berkeley today, close to 85 percent.

"My bragging point is the success of the students who are here," noted Walter Robinson, vice chancellor and director of undergraduate admissions at the school, in 2010. "We bring outstanding students to Berkeley." It is something that once would have been impossible to say without significant qualifiers.

In his superb book *Losing the Race*, the distinguished black linguist John McWhorter, who formerly taught at Berkeley, points out that "the year before preferences were banned at the University of California, exactly one black freshman made honors at the UC San Diego. But in 1999 after the ban, 20 percent of the honors freshmen at San Diego were black. The reason was that black students who formerly were admitted to the flagship schools—UC Berkeley and UCLA—under the bar, now placed into fine second-tier schools like UC San Diego. This is not resegregation but reshuffling, and those who fail to see progress in it are saying no as a gesture, not out of sincere concern."

I know McWhorter and, on the subject of racial preferences and their psychic consequences, no one speaks with greater authority. Though he is today acknowledged to be one of the leading authorities in his field, with multiple awards and honors to prove it, he vividly describes how it was when he learned he'd been admitted as an undergraduate to Stanford on a minority quota. "I went ahead and earned my degree," he wrote, "but I was never able to be as proud of getting into Stanford as my classmates could be. After all, growing up as I did, how much of an achievement can I truly say it was to have been a good enough *black* person to be admitted, while my colleagues had been considered good enough *people* to be admitted."

Later, applying for teaching positions at prestigious universities, he found that "affirmative action repeatedly saved me from coping with the rigors of the job market. . . . I am often congratulated on my career, but the sad fact is that as much as I enjoy my job in many ways, I will never get beyond the sense of diminishment in having gotten it to such an extent 'through the back door.' I got tenure after four and a half years instead of seven, having been rather obsessively productive and having become rather well-known in my specialty. Yet it was perfectly obvious that in the back of most minds was 'Of course he got tenure—they wouldn't dare deny tenure to a black person unless he was absolutely hopeless,' and they were quite right."

In the end, there is no way to change that or any of the rest, but one: Scotch the whole ugly business, root and branch, so that all accomplishment is understood to have been justly earned. Absolutely, let's promote early childhood education, if that can be shown to be effective, as well as tutoring and job training programs for those in the minority community eager to get a leg up. But for the good of everyone, we've got to end, abolish, forever rule out programs that discriminate against anyone on the basis of race or ethnicity.

McWhorter, as it happens, is also a gifted singer, and I'll never forget something he once told me. His proudest achievement while working as a professor at Berkeley, he said, was getting accepted into a Bay Area opera company. Why? For once "I could be absolutely sure I was being judged solely on the merits."

BOOKER T. WASHINGTON
THE NEGLECTED PROPHET

For liberals defending affirmative action—or, for that matter, arguing just about any other aspect of contemporary race relations, from higher rates of black criminality to the extreme sensitivity of many blacks to perceived slights—slavery is the ultimate trump card. And frankly, aimed as it is at casting their opponents as latter-day Simon Legrees, it can be a hell of an effective one. As every American schoolchild learns before mastering the multiplication tables, human bondage is the great, ineradicable American sin. The very thought that our forebears could have tolerated it (and in many cases defended its existence with their lives) sends the modern mind reeling, for the gruesome particulars never lose their emotional force: the hunting and capture of free and independent human souls in West Africa; the nightmar-ish-beyond-description Middle Passage; the ripping asunder of families on the slave block; the barbarism of overseers and slave hunters; the miserable living conditions; and the denial generation after generation of access to that aspect of human experience, education—even basic literacy—that gives rise to hope for a better life.

Preference supporters cite all these and more in justifying their insistence that blacks continue to need special breaks to "catch up"; and so do those equally adamant but, thankfully somewhat fewer, arguing the case for the ultimate victimhood payoff, reparations.

All of it is predicated on the notion that slavery locked people into a state of near-permanent paralysis. Not to put too fine a point on it, but that is not merely a lie, but an especially despicable one that might have been designed with the explicit intention of fostering helplessness and despair. It is ludicrous even on an anecdotal basis, since we can all reel off the names of countless black people who've achieved great success and renown in this country, from Paul Robeson and Colin Powell to Oprah and Condoleeza Rice, the overwhelming majority of whom are themselves descended from slaves. Indeed, the entirety of this book could be devoted to the tales of the family histories of super-achievers whose forebears arrived on this continent in chains.

But of course the race mongers insist these are exceptions to the melancholy rule. They will argue all day that the material and spiritual poverty that undermines so many in urban America—the aimlessness and lack of ambition, the indifference to education, the rampant fatherlessness, all of it—is traceable to the evil of slavery.

Powerful and emotionally resonant as such an argument is at first blush, and even plausible-sounding, it is readily revealed as inept in its reading of both history and human behavior. I've found the quickest, no-muss, no-fuss response to such a claim it is to point out something almost no liberal, black or white, ever seems to know: "Even in the antebellum era, when slaves often weren't permitted to wed, most black children lived with a biological mother and father," Jason Riley observed in the *Wall Street Journal*. "During Reconstruction and up until the 1940s, 75% to 85% of black children lived in two-parent families." Indeed, as recently as 1965, when the historic Voting Rights Act was signed, the black illegitimacy rate was 24 percent, a mere third of what it is now. Couldn't be! you're likely to hear, at which point you can note that the latter statistic comes directly from the legendary report *The Negro Family: The Case for National Action* written by then-assistant secretary of labor and future Sen. Daniel Patrick Moynihan (D-NY). In fact, in 1965, Moynihan was alarmed because black out-of-wedlock births were so much higher than they'd been earlier in the century. "The welfare state has done to black Americans what slavery couldn't do, what Jim Crow couldn't do, what the harshest racism couldn't do," the eminent black economist Walter Williams sums up. "And that is to destroy the black family."

Counterintuitive as it seems, the evidence is overwhelming that at a time when black people were systematically subjected to the most stringent and dehumanizing imaginable discrimination, self-respect and self-reliance were far more the norm in black America than is the case today. The victim mindset did not take full hold until the modern era, *after* the key civil rights battles had been won. Before then, although excuses for failure were all too readily at hand, self-pity was simply a luxury that almost no one could afford. Even in a segregated South where so many were consigned to squalor, there were to be found many vibrant black communities.

"Hard as the laws were on African Americans," observes a contemporary researcher into black life in turn-of-the-century Mount Airy, North Carolina "African Americans set about forming their businesses, schools, churches, communities, and universities. They formed strong family, church, and community bonds. Several black communities developed in Surry County. The most notable is perhaps the community that developed on Needmore Street in Mount Airy. Today called Virginia Street, Needmore began to develop near the close of the 1800s. It soon became a thriving black community (with) entertainment halls, restaurants, churches, cleaners, funeral parlors, barber shops, boarding houses, schools, and more."

A 1913 University of Georgia study, *The Negroes of Athens, Georgia*, detailed the daily life of eight black neighborhoods in that city, in which "the whole range of Negro life is well represented." Largely composed of "home-owning laborers" working as carpenters, brick masons, cobblers, plumbers, barbers, and mechanics, the black community also boasted doctors, nurses, lawyers, teachers, and the first black woman dentist in Georgia.

Nowhere were former slaves and their offspring more entrepreneurial than in the Greenwood district of Tulsa, Oklahoma, which became known as "Negro Wall Street." Benefiting from the area's oil boom, Greenwood produced its own cadre of millionaires, as well as an array of other business owners, professional men, and two successful newspapers. That the community was laid waste in 1921 by one of the worst race riots in American history, leaving 39 dead and unspeakable devastation, is evidence of not only the racial climate of the time, but the spirit it took to thrive despite it.

That spirit reflected the ethic that largely held sway in black America then, one embodied by the most renowned black man of the era, Booker T. Washington.

Washington is a largely forgotten man these days, or at least an overlooked one, which is a shame. "Whatever happened to Booker T. Washington?" a feisty octogenarian friend of my wife's put it to her one day, "Why aren't kids even taught about him anymore, the way we were?"

I know what he meant. When I was a kid, a generation after my wife's friend, Washington was the civil rights pioneer about whom we heard the most, along with the peanut guy, George Washington Carver. Both ex-slaves, they'd overcome extraordinary odds to achieve international renown in their fields—education and agricultural science, respectively—but, more importantly, stood as moral exemplars and models of dedication, perseverance and the resilience of the human spirit.

Still, there's no mystery at all about why the name Booker T. now more readily summons up a sixties R&B band that helped shape the Memphis soul sound than the founder of the Tuskegee Institute. What happened to Booker T. Washington is history—specifically, black history—and the fact he no longer passes muster in the version taught in today's America.

Rather, it is Washington's contemporary and rival, W.E.B. Du Bois, whom posterity has anointed the greatest black man of that long-ago age, casting him as a proud and principled black man in contrast to Washington's ever-eager-to-please glorified house Negro, and as a tireless and uncompromising fighter for his people's rights where Washington tirelessly lived up to his nickname, the Great Accommodator.

But, of course, history always has its contemporary uses, and never more so than in the volatile realm of race relations. In fact, both Washington and Du Bois were extraordinary and highly complex men—and they were more in agreement than is generally allowed.

Yet even if they are defined strictly by their dramatically different approaches to the terrible evils Southern blacks faced two generations after the Civil War—legally mandated and violently enforced segregation and denial of basic rights—Washington gets a bum rap. True enough, in the end, more than half a century later, it was a version of the militancy advocated by Du Bois (practiced with such brilliance by Martin Luther King and his contemporaries) that would force the issue and win the day legally, signaling the beginning of the end of America's brutal and dehumanizing system of apartheid. Still, even at this distance, there was much in Washington's plan that was also far seeing and wise. Idealist that he was, he was profoundly practical, with an unerring grasp of human nature. Even as he labored to improve his people's lot in the dismal present, he was anticipating a future in which his convictions—about industry and thrift as the foundation of self-respect—would have well served millions today consigned to society's margins.

In this sense, the philosophical conflict between these two men has echoed down through the ages. And in key respects, the abandonment of Washington, and the contempt in which his views are held, may truly be said to constitute a road tragically not taken.

Like most highly successful, self-made men, Washington's faith in himself was absolute. This is abundantly apparent in his remarkable autobiography, *Up from Slavery*, which on its publication in 1901 cemented his reputation as an international figure. The book is extraordinary partly because so, too, was his story—that of a boy born in a Virginia slave shack who went on to walk with presidents and kings. But, more than that, it is the force of the man's views that leaps from the page, as well as the understanding that there's to be no glossing over of difficult truths—especially those having to do with the challenges facing black people not just in his lifetime, but well into the future.

Very early on, for instance, Washington wrote poignantly of the very day he and his fellow slaves finally achieved their long dreamt of freedom, with the reading by a Union officer of the Emancipation Proclamation on the veranda of their plantation's "big house." He observed that "for some minutes there was great rejoicing, and thanksgiving, and wild scenes of

ecstasy. But . . . the wild rejoicing on the part of the emanci-
pated colored people lasted but for a brief period, for I noticed
that by the time they returned to their cabins there was a
change in their feelings. The great responsibility of being free,
of having charge of themselves, of having to think and plan for
themselves and their children, seemed to take possession of
them. It was very much like suddenly turning a youth of 10 or
12 years out into the world to provide for himself. . . . Was it
any wonder that within a few hours the wild rejoicing ceased
and a feeling of deep gloom seemed to pervade the slave quarters? To some it seemed that, now that they were in actual possession of it, freedom was a more serious thing than they had
expected to find it. Some of the slaves were 70 or 80 years old;
their best days were gone. They had no strength with which to
earn a living in a strange place and among strange people, even
if they had been sure where to find a new place of abode. To
this class the problem seemed especially hard. . . . Gradually,
one by one, stealthily at first, the older slaves began to wander
from the slave quarters back to the 'big house' to have a whis-
pered conversation with their former owners as to the future."

The vivid picture Washington went on to paint of life for
liberated blacks in the postwar South is full of such surprising
detail. But it is his self-portrait that is most compelling. The
child of a devoted mother and a white father whose identity he
would never know, he faced as desolate a future as any young
black in that gruesome time. He didn't even have a last name
until he chose one for himself. But he had a work ethic that was
nothing short of ferocious. "I had learned from somebody that
the way to begin to read was to learn the alphabet," he writes
of his ninth year, "so I tried in all the ways I could think of to
learn it—all of course without a teacher, for I could find no one
to teach me. At that time there was not a single member of my
race anywhere near us who could read, and I was too timid to

approach any of the white people. In some way, within a few weeks, I mastered the greater portion of the alphabet." As a teen, working in the West Virginia salt furnaces, and later as a house servant, he continued his own rudimentary self-education; then, hearing of the existence of the Hampton Normal and Agricultural Institute, which had been established at the outset of the Civil War by Northerners for ex-slaves, he set out in ragged clothes and nearly penniless for its Hampton Roads, Virginia "campus." He so excelled that six years later, when the Alabama Legislature authorized modest funds for a similar institution in that state, Washington, at 24, was appointed to create it from scratch—a mammoth undertaking he pursued with customary zeal.

Emulating the Hampton program, the school he named Tuskegee offered a mix of basic academics and practical manual training, an education for "the head, the heart, and the hands." While its stress on agricultural training and working-class skills like carpentry and bricklaying, as opposed to a program of pure academics, would later be one of the indictments in the case against Washington, he saw it as essential to what he frankly called the necessary "uplift" of the race. As he wrote of his approach at Tuskegee, "the whole future of the Negro rested largely upon the question as to whether or not he should make himself, through his skill, intelligence, and character, of such undeniable value to the community in which he lived that the community could not dispense with his presence. . . . Any individual who learned to do something better than anybody else—learned to do a common thing in an uncommon manner—had solved his problem, regardless of the color of his skin." He offered as an example the experience of one of the school's graduates who, unlike white farmers in the area, had been trained in the most advanced agricultural methods. As a result, Washington said he "produced 266 bushels of sweet potatoes from an acre of ground, in a community where the average production had been only 49 bushels to the acre. . . . The white farmers in the neighborhood respected him, and came to him for ideas regarding the raising of sweet potatoes." He added that "my theory of education for the Negro would not, for example, confine him for all time to farm life—to the production of the best and the most sweet potatoes—but that, if he succeeded in this line of industry, he could lay the foundations upon which his children and grandchildren could grow to higher and more important things in life."

What he was suggesting, indeed, was a rural Southern equivalent of the experience of Jewish and Italian immigrants in the urban North, in which the children and grandchildren of garment workers and bricklayers became doctors, businessmen, and entrepreneurs.

Washington made clear that such an emphasis was grounded in the necessity, as he saw it, to impress upon the South's rural black population the dignity of honest labor, something that had been largely undermined by slavery. Indeed, reflecting on what he'd seen with his own youthful eyes, he wrote that "the whole machinery of slavery was so constructed as to cause labor, as a rule, to be looked upon as a badge of degradation, of inferiority. Hence labor was something that both races on the slave plantation sought to escape."

Moreover, he had also witnessed much during the period after the war that left him keenly aware of the threat posed by that legacy—augmented by well-intentioned but destructive governmental policies—to black self-reliance. His account of what he saw during a prolonged stay in early 1870s Washington, D.C., for example, could almost have been written last week. "[T]he city was crowded with colored people, many of whom had recently come from the South. A large proportion of these people had been drawn to Washington because they felt that they could lead a life of ease there. Others had secured minor government positions, and still another large class was there in the hope of securing Federal positions. A number of colored men—some of them very strong and brilliant—were in the House of Representatives at that time, and one, the Hon. B. K. Bruce, was in the Senate. All this tended to make Washington an attractive place for members of the colored race. . . . I took great interest in studying the life of our people there closely at that time. I found that while among them there was a large element of substantial, worthy citizens, there was also a superficiality about the life of a large class that greatly alarmed me. I saw young colored men who were not earning more than four dollars a week spend two dollars or more for a buggy on Sunday to ride up and down Pennsylvania Avenue, in order that they might try to convince the world that they were worth thousands. I saw other young men who received seventy-five or one hundred dollars per month from the Government, who were in debt at the end of every month. . . . Among a large class there seemed to be a dependence upon the Government for every conceivable thing. The members of this class had little ambition to create a position for themselves, but wanted the Federal officials to create one for them. How many times I wished then, and have often wished since, that by some power of magic I might remove the great bulk of these people into the country districts and plant them upon the soil, upon the solid and never deceptive foundation of Mother Nature, where all nations and races that have ever succeeded have gotten their start, a start that at first may be slow and toilsome, but one that nevertheless is real."

It was in 1895, 15 years into his tenure at Tuskegee, that Washington exploded on the national consciousness. Tapped to deliver a brief address before an audience of the nation's leading business leaders at the Atlanta Cotton States and International Exposition—an unprecedented honor for a black man in the post-Civil War South—he forcefully restated his philosophy that blacks "shall prosper in proportion as we learn to dignify and glorify common labor . . . that there is as much dignity in tilling a field as in writing a poem"; and urged his influential listeners to invest in Southern businesses and industries to take advantage of the region's abundant black labor force—"the most patient, faithful, law-abiding, and unresentful people that the world has seen"—rather than rely on workers "of foreign birth and strange tongue and habits."

Indeed, the speech included a passage that might have been taken as a warning—or a threat: "Nearly sixteen millions of hands will aid you in pulling the load upward, or they will pull against you the load downward. We shall constitute one-third and more of the ignorance and crime of the South, or one-third [of] its intelligence and progress; we shall contribute one-third to the business and industrial prosperity of the South, or we shall prove a veritable body of death, stagnating, depressing, retarding every effort to advance the body politic."

Still, it was generally upbeat about the future of the region, concluding with a flourish that the future would bring "a blotting out of sectional differences and racial animosities and suspicions, in a determination to administer absolute justice, in a willing obedience among all classes to the mandates of law. This, coupled with our material prosperity, will bring into our beloved South a new heaven and a new earth."

Nonetheless, it was a couple of passages in the middle for which, more than a century later, the speech is still remembered; the ones that are invariably cited by those who today cast Washington as the proto-typical Uncle Tom. Reasserting his hope that the races come to share common commercial interests, he added that "In all things that are purely social we can be as separate as the fingers, yet one as the hand in all things essential to mutual progress." And later: "The wisest among my race understand that the agitation of questions of social equality is the extremist folly, and that progress in the enjoyment of all the privileges that will come to us must be the result of severe and constant struggle rather than of artificial forcing. . . . It is important and right that all privileges of the law be ours, but it is vastly more important that we be prepared for the exercise of these privileges."

This naked attempt to reassure white Southerners that, in essence, blacks would know and respect their place, with all that entailed legally, morally, and emotionally, could hardly be more repugnant to the contemporary sensibility. Lest we forget, the speech was delivered just a year before the Supreme Court's infamous *Plessy v. Ferguson* decision, giving legal sanction to the fraudulent abomination of "separate but equal" and completing the rollback of black rights that, in the aftermath of the Civil War, had briefly seemed assured.

But it is also worth noting, as Washington does at length in his book, that at the time the speech was celebrated as an enormous breakthrough by leading figures and editorialists in the North as well as the South. "I have heard the great orators of many countries," James Creelman wrote in the now-defunct *New York World* newspaper, "but not even Gladstone himself could have pleaded a cause with more consummate power than did this angular Negro, standing in a nimbus of sunshine, surrounded by the men who once fought to keep his race in bondage." Added President Grover Cleveland, one of the era's leading progressives, in a personal letter, "Your words cannot fail to encourage all who wish well for your race."

In fact, in the aftermath of the Atlanta address, Washington was lauded everywhere as an embodiment of hope and racial conciliation. It was hardly for nothing that a speaker's bureau offered him the unheard of fee of $50,000 for his signature on a contract or that offers of honorary degrees started rolling in from almost every prominent institution of higher learning in America, from Harvard on down.

Hardly incidentally, among the great many from whom he heard after the Atlanta speech was William Edward Burghardt Du Bois, who wrote, "Let me heartily congratulate you upon your phenomenal success in Atlanta—it was a word fitly spoken." Though far from the highest praise the speech elicited, there is no reason to believe it was insincere. For while there were those in the black community who publicly worried about Washington's seeming comfort with the racial status quo, mainly church leaders and academics, at that juncture Du Bois was not among them. In fact, he and the older man got on well enough that several years later Washington offered him a teaching position at Tuskegee.

Superficially, the two had much in common. Born 12 years after Washington in 1868 to a black mother and half-white father he would scarcely know, Du Bois also grew up lacking all but the bare material essentials. Yet he, too, was intellectually precocious, and determined from an early age to not go unnoticed by the world.

Yet in other, more crucial ways, their backgrounds were nearly as different as those of two black men coming of age in the second half of 19th century America could have been— and it is this that would set the stage for much that would follow. Where Washington lived his first nine years in bondage, Du Bois grew up in the overwhelmingly white community of Great Barrington, Massachusetts, and from his own account, experienced almost no racial prejudice. Encouraged early on by white teachers who recognized his enormous potential, he mastered Greek and Latin in high school, then went on to earn degrees from the historically black Fisk University in Nashville and Harvard, having attended the latter on scholarship. After doing graduate work at the University of Berlin and traveling widely in Europe, Du Bois returned to Cambridge in 1895, where he became the first black to earn a Harvard Ph.D. in sociology.

Then as now, a Ph.D. invariably led to a teaching career, and the ambitious Du Bois began his at Wilberforce University in Ohio, quickly moving on to the University of Pennsylvania, and then to Atlanta University, where he established the school's Department of Social Work. Along the way, he published widely, poetry as well as learned papers in his field.

He was, in short, and very proudly, an intellectual. And fittingly, his attack on Booker T. Washington, when it came, was in a volume of elegant essays. Titled *The Souls of Black Folk*, it was published three years after *Up from Slavery*. It begins by paying the great man due deference, terming him "the one recognized spokesman of his ten million followers, and one of the most notable figures in a nation of seventy millions." Du Bois also allows that Washington "has had to walk warily . . . for he is dealing with the one subject of deepest sensitiveness to that section" and credits him with having publicly acknowledged that race prejudice is "eating away the vitals of the South."

But he soon moves in for the kill, attacking the two most fundamental aspects of Washington's agenda.

- First, "Mr. Washington's program practically accepts the alleged inferiority of the Negro races. . . . In the history of nearly all other races and peoples the doctrine preached at such crises has been that manly self-respect is worth more than lands and houses, and that a people who voluntarily surrender such respect, or cease striving for it, are not worth civilizing."
- Second, he takes on Washington's emphasis on manual education, writing that to the sage of Tuskegee

"the picture of a lone black boy poring over a French grammar amid the weeds and dirt of a neglected home soon seemed . . . the acme of absurdities. One wonders what Socrates and St. Francis of Assisi would say to this."

Du Bois concludes with an alternative vision of the future, writing that his fellow blacks "do not expect to see the bias and prejudices of years disappear at the blast of a trumpet; but they are absolutely certain that the way for a people to gain their reasonable rights is not by voluntarily throwing them away and insisting that they do not want them; that the way for a people to gain respect is not by continually belittling and ridiculing themselves; that, on the contrary, Negroes must insist continually, in season and out of season, that voting is necessary to modern manhood, that color discrimination is barbarism, and that black boys need education as well as white boys."

This, needless to say, is the Du Bois so highly esteemed today, the one whose words seem to have been uncannily borne out by events five and six decades later.

In fact, the stirring words did not always reflect the essence of a complex and contradictory man—who was, for one thing, far more elitist than democrat, believing only a "Talented Tenth" of blacks were fit for a college education—but the history books, written by his fellow winners, tend to skim lightly over the messy parts. What counts, in the contemporary consensus, is that on the big issue—how best to confront intractable white racism—he was right, and Washington was wrong.

Nor did Du Bois, though very much an idea man, simply confine himself to the realm of social theory. Two years after the publication of *The Souls of Black Folk*, he joined with other black intellectuals who shared his opinion that Washington had been compromised by his reliance on wealthy white contributors to found the Niagara Movement, with the professed aim of challenging Washington's leadership of black America. Four years after that, in 1909, Du Bois was one of the founders of the NAACP, assuming editorship of its magazine, the *Crisis*. In this capacity and others, he spent most of the rest of what would be a very long life aggressively agitating against anti-black bigotry.

Washington, for his part, had a deeply ambivalent relationship with his rival. While bitterly resenting the attacks of Du Bois and his allies—so much so that he is said at one point to have hired spies to trail Du Bois—Washington sometimes helped finance their pro-civil rights activities behind the scenes. Although Washington never publicly disavowed his Atlanta speech, he shared the·integrationists' ultimate goals, if not all their tactics. When he died suddenly in 1915, at 59, after collapsing in New York during a speaking and fund-raising tour (it was reported at the time that the probable cause was nervous exhaustion brought on by overwork), there was widespread shock and grief. He was almost universally hailed, as the *New York Times* had it, as the "foremost teacher and leader of the negro race" and, per Theodore Roosevelt, as an American patriot who was "one of the most useful citizens of our land."

But Du Bois, for his part, retreated not an inch. "Booker T. Washington was the greatest Negro leader since Frederick Douglass, and the most distinguished man, white or black, who has come out of the South since the Civil War," he wrote in the *Crisis*. "On the other hand, in stern justice, we must lay on the soul of this man, a heavy responsibility for the consummation of Negro disfranchisement, the decline of the Negro college and the firmer establishment of color caste in this land."

Du Bois died in August 1963, six months into his 96th year, and the way that sad event came to the world's notice could hardly have been more dramatic: It was announced by NAACP head Roy Wilkins during the massive civil rights rally remembered for Martin Luther King's "I Have a Dream" speech. For many in the stunned crowd, the old man was at the time an even greater hero than King himself.

But it is also the case that Du Bois had lived to be embittered and disappointed in America, in ways that Washington, the former slave, would have found startling and appalling. Increasingly a man of the left as he grew older, by the post-World War II era he was an enthusiastic admirer of Joseph Stalin and an all-around Soviet apologist, finally joining the Communist Party in 1961, and soon after abandoning his native country altogether to live out his remaining few years in Ghana.

The significance of this last to his work as a civil rights activist is not as remote as it might seem. Du Bois was a man of passionate belief, but not always a practical or especially thoughtful one. The noble idea he so assiduously pursued, and for which he is still justly celebrated—full and unequivocal racial equality—in the end became a matter of law only as a result of the dirty work of political give and take; and even then largely because a new electronic media had laid bare beyond all denying the ugliness, viciousness and cruelty of the way things were.

What Du Bois never accounted for, and indeed had no place in his intellectual universe, was what Washington made the center of his: human nature. And ultimately, Washington's view has been borne out by events. For all the remarkable successes of the civil rights revolution, its great misstep has been in failing to recognize that it is not only the laws on the books, but behavior and cultural norms—attitudes about work, frugality, marriage and family—that are essential to self-respect and life success. What was needed at that crucial moment was a synthesis of Du Bois's focus on ending what remained of the past's collective victimization with, going forward, Washington's own individual accountability. Notwithstanding the progress we've made on race in the decades since, that fact continues to haunt black America.

Reading Washington, one is repeatedly struck by his startling prescience. There is a "class of colored people who make a business of keeping the troubles, the wrongs, and the hardships of the Negro race before the public," he observed in 1911, more than half a century before anyone had heard of Jesse Jackson or Al Sharpton. "Having learned that they are able to make a living out of their troubles, they have grown into the settled habit of advertising their wrongs—partly because they want sympathy and partly because it pays. Some of these people do not want the Negro to lose his grievances, because they do not want to lose their jobs."

Indeed, the Sharptons and Jacksons of this world are not his heirs, but Du Bois's; cruel as were the times in which he lived, Washington continually found reason to expect so much better. "Every persecuted individual and race should get much consolation out of the great human law, which is universal and eternal, that merit, no matter under what skin found, is, in the long run, recognized and rewarded," he wrote in *Up from Slavery*. "This I have said here, not to call attention to myself as an individual, but to the race to which I am proud to belong."

IT'S NOT BRAINS, STUPID, IT'S CULTURE

Not long after I graduated from journalism school in the early seventies, I got a call from a classmate I'll call Sam. He'd gone to work for a Hearst tabloid in Chicago, the now long-defunct *Chicago Today*, and he had a strange story to tell from his first week there; strange, at least, to our white, middle-class liberal ears. It seems that as a rookie he was working the graveyard shift, and the night before, in the wee hours, he'd been assigned to accompany police investigating a shooting at the Robert Taylor Homes, completed just a decade earlier to provide good, affordable housing for the urban poor but already in decay and wracked by violence. Arriving with the cops, Sam was startled by what he saw: *Everyone was awake.* "Here it was 2 a.m. and it was like it was the middle of afternoon," he recalled recently, when I reminded him of that long-ago night. "In almost every apartment, the lights were blazing, the TV was on and everyone was up—parents, kids, old people. It was like I'd entered a completely different universe!"

And of course he had. Like most from his class and background, he lived in a world marked by a certain order and self-discipline, one in which it was the rule that the young pursue their education with some degree of seriousness and, moving on to the working world, that they perform reliably and well. The one he'd entered, with its broken elevators and graffiti-marred halls, was . . . what would be the term? Chaotic? Anarchic? Depraved?

And what was abundantly, tragically clear is that almost every young person in it was doomed.

Not that Sam felt comfortable saying that, except privately—then or even now. (Note the pseudonym.) While it is customary for even liberal commentators to note that conditions of inner-city life "breed hopelessness and despair" and "trap" the underclass in a "cycle of poverty," it is risky in the extreme to focus on specific behaviors or, even more so, to suggest remedial measures that might actually stand a chance of altering the lamentable status quo. These are invariably construed as "harsh," mean-spirited" and "draconian." Even 1996's welfare reform, (as embodied in the for once-aptly-named Personal Responsibility and Work Opportunity Act)—in retrospect, so obviously sensible in taking on a system that actively *discouraged* work and kept men from their families—was widely attacked at the time for its many purported cruelties, and only got signed (on the third try) because Bill Clinton needed it to get reelected. In general, in multicultural America it is far safer to condemn the manifold "inequities" confronting inner-city blacks than to risk being seen as insensitive. Even Bill Cosby, as bullet proof as you get in this country after a long and exemplary run as a cross-racial icon, got his head handed to him by black activists and academics for daring to speak up about the all too obvious problems associated with the culture of the black underclass.

The sad truth is that almost no one would be surprised today by what my journalist friend saw 35 years ago; not after all we've learned of such places in the years since. It's all but inescapable now, evident in everything from rap music lyrics to TV shows like *The Wire* and the parade of profanity and violence laced dramas on the big screen.

Even so, an especially up-close-and-personal version of the phenomenon, like 2009's Oscar-winning *Precious*, can still send white, middle-class audiences reeling, as if from a horror film. "To be honest," conceded the film's (black) director, Lee Daniels, to the *New York Times*, "I was embarrassed to show this movie at Cannes. I didn't want to exploit black people. And I wasn't sure I wanted white French people to see our world."

Yet, tellingly, Daniels was just as concerned about how *Precious* would play with black audiences. "They see the film as negative to black women. Black women are the pillar of the family. Black men have left, and how dare I stab at the one thing that's helped."

His concern is understandable, and so is the defensiveness of so many black people. The portrait the film paints of urban underclass culture is devastating. Its ironically named title character, an obese 16-year-old pregnant for the second time by her own father, lives with her nightmarishly abusive mother in Section 8 housing. Illiterate and monosyllabic, she seems to move through life with little more consciousness of the world than her Down syndrome child, her connection to the habits and values of mainstream America tenuous to the point of invisibility. As the *Times* ever so delicately put it, the film "risks reinforcing old stereotypes."

Alas, on the evidence, it is a "stereotype" that is all too prevalent as a reality. This is why this extraordinary film, like similarly unflinching depictions of its harsh truths, gives rise to very dangerous questions: How did it ever come to this? Was it simply a matter of terrible social policy or might there be other factors at play? Which is to say, how much does it have to do with today's version of urban black culture?

In fact, "dangerous" is an understatement; posed with sufficient indelicacy in the public square or even the workplace, such questions are potentially fatal. Anyone else got a theory as to why this massive elephant rumbling through the hallways of the sprawling American edifice is so roundly ignored?

What's odd is that, in other contexts, Americans talk incessantly about culture and the powerful influences it exerts, especially on the impressionable young. Take, for instance, the great Tiger Mom controversy of 2011. Seemingly within a day of the release of the book by Chinese-American Yale law professor Amy Chua recounting how she produced super-achieving daughters via fanatical adherence to the all-work, no-play Chinese style of child rearing, half of middle-class American motherhood was up in arms, defending our more laissez-faire cultural ways.

Or take our current, legitimate obsession with childhood obesity—a phenomenon universally recognized to be a product of cultural shifts involving greater consumption of fast food and less time on the playground. More, as everyone from Michelle Obama to the neighborhood nutritionist readily observes, the problem is especially acute in the black community, where childhood obesity rates approach a staggering 30 percent.

Yet to pose other questions about the impact of the cultural environment on the urban young is absolutely verboten. It's as if the only cause for concern in the depressing existence of Claireece "Precious" Jones was that immense tub of greasy chicken Precious stole from a fast-food joint on the corner.

Indeed, to make an issue of the demonstratively calamitous aspects of black urban culture is in many quarters taken (if sometimes only strategically) as attacking that amorphous thing called black "authenticity," or even as an assault on the rich black cultural tradition in general.

That is nonsense, of course. As Americans, we celebrate our distinct ethnic heritages, and we hardly need Black History Month to remind us of our collective debt to black culture.

Yet it is also true that among vast swaths of the black underclass in America what's been lost is a concomitant reverence for the values and attitudes once held in common across ethnic and racial lines; the ones that cement our bonds as a people. Even the unrepentant Sinophile Amy Chua, badgered by a *Wall Street Journal* interviewer, readily paid obeisance to this idea. "We started off as outsiders together," she said, recalling life with her immigrant parents, "and we discovered America together, becoming Americans in the process. I remember my father working until three in the morning every night, so driven he wouldn't even notice us entering the room. But . . . I also remember Girl Scouts and hula hoops; poetry contests and public libraries; winning a Daughters of the American Revolution essay contest; and the proud, momentous day my parents were naturalized."

Keenly aware that such an attitude is absent in much of urban America—and, more, that underclass neighborhoods seem breeding grounds for moral chaos—we seek explanations. If not underclass culture, what *is* the essence of the problem? In the enforced absence of a vital conversation on the subject, is it any wonder that an unsettling alternative assumption—fed also by the toxin of racial preferences—today has widespread currency in America: That in general black people just aren't as capable as their fellow citizens? Or, worse, as smart?

People of goodwill naturally shrink from such a possibility, and desperately want it not to be so, including many who fear it is. It's not for nothing that Barack Obama's untested "brilliance" was so widely and eagerly proclaimed. Or that a lot of us automatically root for black contestants on *Jeopardy*. Or that we're always glad to find the black astrophysicist Neil deGrasse Tyson holding forth anew on PBS. Or that, for instance, running across former drug dealing rapper/entrepreneur Jay-Z on the same network running mental circles around the left's favorite pseudo-intellectual, Charlie Rose (in especially obsequious, shit-eat-grin mode) is such an unexpected pleasure.

We feel that way, at least in part, because we sense how tough it must be for the vast majority of black people to live down the ugly excesses of the minority. Moreover, most of us know enough smart black people in our own circle to render the notion that blacks as a group might lag behind the rest of us as a matter of biology highly dubious.

Of course, the whole business would have baffled our forebears—not just our inability to candidly address the topic, but the need to have the conversation at all—since most of them simply presumed white racial superiority. To focus on just a handful of the most often cited cases: Jefferson, though his views on the subject were complex and contradictory, notoriously wrote in *Notes on the State of Virginia* that blacks are "inferior to the whites in the endowments of both body and mind." During his debates with Stephen Douglas, Lincoln repeatedly made the point that while he opposed slavery on moral grounds, regarding the races "there must be the position of superior and inferior," and "I as much as any other man am in favor of the superior position being assigned to the white man." Woodrow Wilson not only famously said of *Birth of a Nation* that it "is like writing history with lightning," but added, "my only regret is that it is all so true." Then there was Richard Nixon who, overheard on the secret White House tapes, seems to have swallowed every morsel of it whole, with an added dash of his own special spitefulness and scorn. While conceding "some of them are smart," Nixon said it might take

500 years for blacks to be the equal of whites, and only then after interbreeding." If his Jewish stereotype was arguably more vicious—i.e., "very aggressive and abrasive and obnoxious" and "you can't trust the bastards"—it was not nearly so demeaning.

Then there's the feminist icon Margaret Sanger, founder of Planned Parenthood. Though the fact is invariably minimized in the hagiographic biographies, or airbrushed out altogether, Sanger was an ardent eugenicist, and especially had it in for black people. Envisaging that birth control would bring about "race improvement," in 1930 Sanger launched a "Negro Project" via "an experimental clinic" in Harlem, with the express purpose of ridding the general population of a maximum number of those she considered moral and intellectual undesirables, "human weeds." It would doubtless please her to learn that today, in her hometown of New York City, three of every five black fetuses are aborted; the very result, or at least a good part of it, she envisaged all those years ago.

In fact, the eugenicist theories enjoyed widespread currency in progressive circles during the first part of the last century, endorsed even by Du Bois. "The mass of ignorant Negroes still breed carelessly and disastrously," as he wrote in a 1932 essay in Sanger's *Birth Control Review*, adding that blacks had to "learn that among human races and groups, as among vegetables, quality and not mere quantity really counts."

It goes without saying that, no matter the source, such talk in our own time registers as deeply pernicious, and the reflex is to label anyone who indulges in it as racist—something which in addition to allowing us to avoid dealing with it substantively, often has the further advantage of being generally accurate. Back in the seventies, for instance, there was William Shockley, a certified physics genius, with a Nobel Prize for co-inventing the transistor. Late in his career, Shockley was subject to near-universal condemnation when he began expounding theories about race and IQ that were both shocking and ugly in where they led him; as in his proposing that individuals with IQ's below 100 submit to voluntary sterilization. Daniel J. Kevles, a history of science professor at Yale, summed up the consensus with his observation that Shockley "invited ridicule as a racist and biological ignoramus."

Thirty years later, in 2007, an even better known Nobelist, co-discoverer of DNA and former head of the Human Genome Project James D. Watson, provoked a firestorm after declaring himself in the *London Sunday Times* "inherently gloomy about the prospect of Africa [because] all our social policies are based on the fact that their intelligence is the same as ours—whereas all the testing says not really." With Federation of American Scientists president Henry Kelly calling it "tragic that one of the icons of modern science has cast such dishonour on the profession"—and bloggers on the net, less constrained by collegiality, tossing around references to Nazism—Watson immediately issued a heartfelt apology claiming to have been misquoted, but he was still forced to resign as chancellor of the Cold Spring Harbor Laboratory and from its board of directors.

These days comparisons to Nazism are at once so pervasive and wildly overblown as to be meaningless, the province of zealots devoid of any serious grasp of history. Bush was a Nazi and so is Obama; Israel is a Nazi state, and Arizona is well on its way. As Internet attorney Mike Godwin postulated in Godwin's Rule of Nazi Analogies, any discussion on any subject, if it goes on long enough, will inevitably involve "a comparison being made to Nazis or Hitler."

Still, this is one context where not every such analogy is inherently false. In the muted but widespread presumption of black intellectual inadequacy, there are echoes—sometimes more than echoes—of the thinking of the likes of Alfred

Rosenberg, the Nazi Party's chief racial theorist, and promulgator of the "human racial ladder," which had Jews and blacks on the bottom rung.

Destined to Witness, a remarkable memoir of Germany under the Nazis by Hans J. Massaquoi, should be more than enough to correct any misapprehensions on that score. The son of a German woman and a Liberian diplomat, Massaquoi was seven when Hitler came to power, and somehow he managed to survive in Germany through the entire war, before eventually making it to America, where he became a top editor at *Ebony*. But 60 years later the humiliations of childhood were still stunningly fresh. He writes, for instance, of Herr Dutke, the science teacher he had as a 10-year-old. On one occasion, impressed by the portable radio Dutke designed and showed the class, young Massaquoi went home and started trying to come up with a variation of his own. The following Monday, he arrived at school with "a small three-by-four-inch wooden box into which I had fitted the circuitry and earphone of a crystal set. In principle, my little radio box worked just like Dutke's boxless earphone." His classmates were bowled over, and he expected equal praise from the teacher. Instead, Dutke "berated me for coming up with a clumsy imitation of his own creation and told me not to bring such *Murks* (Hamburg slang for poor workmanship) into his class.

"I was devastated, and so were some of my classmates, who tried to console me after class by telling me that the only thing that made Dutke mad at me was that he couldn't sell me one of his earphones. I was certain that they were partially right but I also knew that there was another, even more important reason for Dutke's rejection of me—the color of my skin.

"My suspicion was soon confirmed. When a pupil referred to my scholastic and athletic abilities to refute Dutke's contention that people of other than 'Aryan blood' were both intellectually and physically inferior, Dutke dressed down the pupil for daring to disagree with him. He then lectured the class that my case was merely the exception that proved the rule, and suggested that whatever 'normal characteristics' I displayed I had definitely inherited from my Aryan parent. Without the slightest consideration of my feelings, he suggested that in my case the last word had not yet been spoken, and that there was still a very good chance that my inferior blood would surface in one form or another. 'There are many ways of being racially inferior,' he argued. 'I wouldn't be at all surprised if your *Klassenkamerad* one day winds up as an antisocial element, such as a criminal or an alcoholic, or if he isn't already susceptible to a host of debilitating diseases.' "

After dismissing the rest of the class, the teacher had one final word for Massaquoi: "Let me tell you something, young man. Don't feel so smug, because after we have finished with the Jews, people like you will be next. That's all I have to say. *Heil Hitler.*"

Given that ugly history, and our own version of apartheid on these shores—not to mention modern America's ecstatic and starry-eyed embrace of diversity—it is understandable that precious few will risk asserting publicly the existence of any inherent differences between racial or ethnic groups at all; at least, any that might be construed as reflecting other than positively on "historically disadvantage groups." Never mind that, consistency be damned, correct thinkers have no trouble at all asserting the inherent *superiority* of those groups. It is fine to observe, for example, that girls are naturally better than boys in English—but perish the thought they're weaker in math or science—*that's* a culturally contrived myth that must be quashed. Indeed, Larry Summers was forced from the presidency of Harvard for daring to suggest that such a thing was even open to discussion. So while anyone with eyes and a cable system with ESPN can clearly see that blacks dominate athletically, God forbid that anyone draw any further conclusions about genetic predispositions.

The contortions some will put themselves through to avoid even the appearance of challenging orthodoxy on this score can be as amusing as they are pitiful. Back in the summer of 1992, I was editing a small magazine for parents of kids involved in youth sports. Since at that moment the Olympic Games were taking place in Barcelona, my colleagues and I hit upon the idea of a piece addressing a question that a perceptive child watching track events might well ask his parents: Why is it that such an overwhelming majority of track stars are black? To suggest how parents might answer it, I called upon a professional ethicist affiliated with a big-time university who, then as now, appeared regularly on TV discoursing on all manner of moral questions. When his piece came in, I was startled to find that he'd basically refused to answer the question. More precisely, he did so in a way that was so timid as to be unpublishable, basically saying that the track stars' speed had nothing to do with their physical selves—they ran fast only as a result of the environment that had produced them. I pointed out to the guy that such a response was unlikely to satisfy even the dullest witted child, especially since the athletes in question came from environments as varied as America's inner cities, the western highlands of Kenya, the suburbs of Toronto and rural Jamaica. He took the piece back, rewrote it and handed it back, saying exactly the same thing in slightly different words. Since he would not, or could not, seriously engage the issue, we ended up killing the piece.

Quite simply, for such a guy, comfortably ensconced in the American academic mainstream, the thought of publicly suggesting that there might be something about black people that makes them run faster—something innate—was nothing short of terrifying; for it inevitably led to the possibility that other traits might be also—notably those that have to do with intellectual achievement.

So the subject, painful and awkward as it might be, remains permanently stashed under the rug. Except we can never completely forget it's there.

One of the few who's frankly addressed the forbidden topic is Dinesh D'Souza in his book *What's So Great About America*. Noting that "equality of rights for individuals has not led to equality of results for groups," he turns his attention to the achievement gap between blacks and their fellow citizens. Starting with the oft cited disparity between the races on the SAT college admissions tests, he asks readers to "envision any test that measures intellectual achievement or economic performance. It may be a reading test given to 15-year-olds, or the law school admission test, or the graduate record exam, or the business school test, or the firefighters test, or the police sergeant test, or the civil service exam. It doesn't matter—you name the test. Now if your chosen test is today administered to a hundred randomly selected members from each of four groups—white, black, Hispanic and Asian-American—I will tell you in advance the result. Whites and Asians will do the best, Hispanics will fall in the middle, and African-Americans, alas, will do the least well."

In this, he implicitly endorses (though later in his book he appears to reject) the thesis most famously—or notoriously—advanced by Richard J. Herrnstein and Charles Murray in their 1994 book, *The Bell Curve*: i.e., that while those of all racial groups are found at all points on the IQ spectrum, on average the IQ of blacks is lower than that of whites or Asians. And since intelligence, the best predictor of real-world success, is a heritable trait, a very great many of low scorers are doomed to lives on society's margins. Though, later on the authors fudged the point somewhat, endorsing the likelihood that "both genes and the environment have something to do" with the measurable distinctions between the intelligence of different ethnic groups, it's a safe bet few book buyers were interested in the subtleties.

To be sure, *The Bell Curve* was one of those best sellers that almost no ordinary people read, since it not only reads like a social science text (down to the many charts and graphs) but is roughly as long as three John Grishams. Nor, presumably, did very many of those in the mainstream press who so vigorous attacked it (or even its relative handful of defenders) read it all the way through either. Not that that gave anyone pause. Although the issue of race doesn't even turn up until chapter 13, temptingly titled "Ethnic Differences in Cognitive Ability," within a week of the book's publication, "R" for "racist" had been attached to it in perpetuity. *Newsweek* called it "frightening stuff"; *New York* magazine, "grist for racism of every variety"; *Time*, "845 pages of provocation with footnotes." Michael Lind of *Harper's* dismissed it as "racialist pseudoscience" and The *New Republic's* Jeffrey Rosen and Charles Lane called it "a chilly synthesis of the work of disreputable race theorists and eccentric eugenicists." Brandeis history professor Jacqueline Jones spoke for most of her academic colleagues in declaring "*The Bell Curve* amounts to hate literature with footnotes."

Reading them close to two decades later, there is no doubting the sincerity of the book's many critics, or the depth of their outrage. The real issue, as most saw it then, and still do today, was the privations America had visited upon black people, from the cruelties of the slave period to the denial of their fundamental humanity for more than a century afterward; and if they still had some catching up to do, that was a debt white America was obligated to pay. Indeed, the ubiquitous Henry

Louis Gates was not alone in seeing in the book's publication an especially sinister design. For, he wrote, were *The Bell Curve* to succeed in persuading policymakers that intelligence is destiny, it would dampen "the enthusiasm of liberals in Congress for the equivalent of a Marshall Plan for our cities," and otherwise justify the canard that social spending was all but pointless. He concluded by paraphrasing what Frederick Douglass said of slavery: "The crimes of discrimination have become discrimination's best defense."

Nonetheless, there is little question the book aroused such ire because it was saying something that a great many people suspected to be true. As Herrnstein and Murray themselves observed in an article just prior to the book's publication, "The private dialogue about race in America is far different from the public one."

Herrnstein and Murray understood that the implications of their work were potentially gruesome: a tragedy for black people and a catastrophe for America. "Biology suggests a grim inevitability," as the eminent sociologist Nathan Glazer noted in a critique of the book, "and if that inevitability means blacks remain in a permanently inferior position in American society, there are good reasons to avoid biology as far as possible."

Glazer's observation is included in *The Bell Curve Wars*, a compendium of essays on the book. It offers a variety of points of view on the subject, from the standard *ad hominem* attacks to respectful partial agreement, and read one after another, they serve to focus the mind. I found myself nodding my head at several essays in particular, not only because what they were saying made sense but because over the years I'd come to respect their authors as honest and fair-minded.

Mickey Kaus, whose essay originally appeared in *The New Republic*, hits Herrnstein and Murray hard, looking to the abundant evidence that undermines the notion that IQ is primarily a matter of heredity. In particular, he points to "the convergence of black and white test scores over the past twenty years, which Murray and Herrnstein agree has been so fast it is 'likely' due to 'environmental changes.'" In fact, he adds, "Murray and Herrnstein admit that if such a trend continues, black and white test scores would 'reach equality sometime in the middle of the twenty-first century.'"

Kaus proceeds to offer examples in which significant environmental change has resulted in dramatic change in test scores, then cites the equivocation of the book's authors themselves to cinch his case. He writes that the best they "can do with the evidence at hand is to declare it 'highly likely' that genes have 'something' to do with racial differences. How much? 'We are resolutely agnostic on that issue,' they say. In other words, the genetic contribution could be 50 percent, it could be 1 percent, or .001 percent, for all they know. Or (though this is not 'likely') it could be zero. A significant role for the environment, however, has been substantiated."

Thomas Sowell is far more generous toward Herrnstein and Murray, whom he respects for their intellectual rigor and seriousness of purpose, and he has nothing but contempt for those of their critics driven by little more than PC-approved thought. Still, his rundown of factors establishing the link between environment and IQ takes Kaus's argument even further. He points out, for instance, that it is not just blacks but also newly arrived European immigrants who scored poorly on measures of abstract reasoning, adding: "So did white mountaineer children in the United States tested back in the early 1930's. So did canal boat children in Britain, and so did rural British children compared to their urban counterparts. . . . In short, groups outside the cultural mainstream of contemporary Western society tend to do their worst on abstract questions, whatever their race may be."

He adds that "perhaps the strongest evidence against a genetic basis for inter-group differences in IQ" is how dramatically certain groups' IQ scores have risen over time, singling out—how's this for a surprise?—American Jews. In fact, it seems that when during World War I IQ tests were taken by Russian-born American soldiers, the overwhelming number of them Jewish, their scores were so low that the creator of the SAT declared they "disprove the popular notion that the Jew is highly intelligent." Yet scores rose dramatically as the recently arrived foreigners became more fully acclimated to American life and culture. Sowell points out that his own research with Italian and Polish Americans found a similar rise in scores over a period of decades. He notes, too, that black women routinely score higher than black men on such tests—hardly comforting for black men, but certainly a refutation of the notion that any intelligence gap could be innate to blacks in general.

Finally, there was a lengthy essay by Orlando Patterson, the noted Jamaican-born sociologist. Since Patterson teaches at Harvard, where taking on liberal orthodoxy on race or anything else is always an adventure, what he has to say is especially risky. For while he has little sympathy for *The Bell Curve*'s take on the heredity issue, he has even less for many of those who rose up with such fury to attack it. Why? Because these are the very same people who with equal obduracy and anger refuse to link even the most destructive problems endemic to the cities to urban black culture. "It is now wholly incorrect politically to even utter the word culture, as an explanation, in any context other than counterattacks against hereditarians," he observes. "Indeed so far has this politically correct position gone that it is not uncommon for persons who even tentatively point to social and cultural deficiencies to be labeled and condemned as racists. . . . We cannot have it both ways. If culture is the savior against the hereditarians and those persuaded by

The Bell Curve, culture must contain the answer as we search for an explanation of the pathological sink into which some 10 million Americans have fallen."

That is more than just simple common sense. It is also hopeful, since culture, unlike heredity, can with strenuous effort be overcome. But as he suggests, such a process must entail honesty about the nature and depths of the deficits to be faced.

"You were born poor," the ever-insightful Daniel Patrick Moynihan once wrote Lyndon Johnson. "You were brought up poor. Yet you came of age full of ambition, energy, and ability. Because your mother and father gave it to you. The richest inheritance any child can have is a stable, loving, disciplined family life."

Moynihan also suggested that public policy might help foster such personal discipline on a grand scale—if only those across the political spectrum saw it as their business to join in that essential goal. The "central conservative truth is that it is culture, not politics, that determines the success of a society," as he observed in his famous dictum, and "the central liberal truth is that politics can change a culture and save it from itself."

But that was a different time and a different liberalism. The one we've got today appears dedicated to *not* facing up to the depravity rampant in our inner cities.

"The mayor, preachers, City Council members, county commissioners, teachers, judges, social workers and other outsiders cannot save black children," wrote the *St. Petersburg Times's* columnist Bill Maxwell of today's platitudinous liberal officialdom, in a strikingly brave piece following another senseless murder in that Florida city's violent Midtown neighborhood in March 2011. "These children will be saved or lost based on the moral and ethical environment in their homes. The adults in these children's lives must teach, without apology or equivocation, what is acceptable and what is unacceptable, what is admirable and what is contemptible."

"And so it goes," wrote one local reader in response, "on and on and on and on again—a Mobius of drugs, death, and disgrace. Why do blacks accept this behavior?"

Why, indeed? And why does society at large? Both because the problem is so overwhelming, and its cause is so frighteningly clear: underclass culture itself.

The Robert Taylor Homes my friend visited all those years ago were, like his newspaper, finally closed down. This happened only after the turn of the 21st century and the chaos had reached such hellish proportions it could no longer be tolerated even by Chicago's Democrat machine: 95 percent unemployment, routine arson, drug gangs running rampant. In one especially harrowing weekend, 28 people were killed.

Since then, there have been a number of studies focusing on what happened at the Robert Taylor Homes. The most notable was the 2001 study commissioned by the *Journal of the Illinois State Historical Society* titled "What Went Wrong with Public Housing in Chicago?" It is an amazing document: 20 tightly written pages long, including footnotes, its scholarly author examined in detail every one of the factors he regarded as crucial, from the design of the buildings and absence of green space to the way political patronage was allocated and the manner other key decisions were made.

But there is not a word about the culture of those who turned what was once an idealistic vision into a hell on Earth.

LET'S PRETEND NO. 2
FATHERS DON'T MATTER

On the evidence of what he writes in *Up from Slavery*, Booker T. Washington was distinctly not the sort of touchy-feely guy so much in vogue today. Perhaps that is why his brief, out-of-the-blue but deeply felt mentions of his children are so poignant. "Years ago I resolved that because I had no ancestry myself I would leave a record of which my children would be proud, and which might encourage them to still higher effort," he wrote at one point. "One of the most satisfactory letters that I have ever received from anyone came to me from Booker, last summer. . . . 'My Dear Papa: Before you left home you told me to work at my trade half of each day. I like my work so much that I want to work at my trade all day. Besides, I want to earn all the money I can, so that when I go to another school I shall have money to pay my expenses. Your son, Booker.'"

As it happens, the very day I read that, I ran across something in the *New York Post* that was a mirror image of Washington's prideful look at his son; admiring remarks made more than a century later by a son—super successful TV producer (and Charlie Sheen antagonist) Chuck Lorre, about how much he owed his father. Lorre's father, Robert Levine, owned a Long Island luncheonette and, as his son told an interviewer, "Against my will, he taught me how to work. I bitched and complained and moaned. I'd get up at five o'clock in the morning and go in with him and put together 18 New York newspapers. . . . The work was really backbreaking and he just did it. And he never called in sick a day in his life. A remarkable man. His work ethic was astonishing. His willingness to suit up, shut up and show up."

This, of course, is what fathers do, at least the good ones: They instruct by example. Instilling a strong work ethic is simply part of the job description, which is to live with integrity even when it's not easy; and so, too, even more vitally, to treat women with tenderness and respect, and to make one's children the absolutely highest priority.

This is why, unquestionably, the single greatest tragedy for black people in today's America—indeed, the greatest calamity since slavery itself—is that scarcely one in four black fathers is on the scene to make the kinds of loving observations that came so naturally across the years to Washington and Lorre. That adds up to roughly 40 million black kids living today in homes without fathers.

In the abstract, we know what this means. So routinely bruited about are the dire consequences associated with growing up in such circumstances that even casual fans of social science can reel them off without crib notes: the massively enhanced risks of academic failure, drug use and criminality; the higher rates of depression, early sexual activity and adolescent parenthood; the vastly increased odds of poverty and social instability. Indeed, the poverty rate of married-couple families in America is one-fifth that of female-headed families with children.

"The statistics are so jaw-dropping that not giving up an illegitimate child for adoption ought to be considered child abuse," observed Ann Coulter with characteristic unvarnished bluntness.

Up close and personal, the particulars are often nothing short of wrenching. The Manhattan Institute's Heather Mac Donald writes of a 16-year-old honor student in Chicago named Derrion Albert who was murdered after getting caught in an after-school battle between rival gangs; savagely beaten and stomped on by gangbangers, as dozens of other teens looked on. None of the four youths arrested for the killing had a father in his life, and neither did the victim. As one observer noted, the murdered boy's father saw him just once, "the day he was born, and the next time when he was in a casket."

Yet for all that, precious few in the public arena, including what passes for black leadership, are willing to address the crisis with the urgency it so clearly merits. Even the Conference of National Black Churches, representing 50,000 black denominations and 30 million people (and so presumably interested more than most in their spiritual and material well-being), has dodged the fatherlessness question, focusing instead on the always safe issue of tax cuts for the wealthy.

My advice to them, and to all whose heads are similarly planted in the ground, is to take a few hours off each week from their busy schedules to catch Maury Povich's show on the tube. This suggestion is not entirely facetious. A decade ago, laid up for a couple of weeks with a bad back, I watched *Maury* regularly, and it was the very definition of an education—a more in depth and horrifying look at the tragedy of life without fathers in America's inner cities than anything to be found in any congressional study or sociological text.

Povich's show, these days called simply *Maury*, is syndicated. In the New York market it's on every weekday morning at nine on WPIX, a schlock bazaar that also runs *Jerry Springer*, along with the Mets and a slew of second-rate sitcom reruns. Povich, the husband of former anchor babe Connie Chung, was once a reputable journalist, something he came by honestly, since his own father, the unfortunately named Shirley, for decades labored for the *Washington Post* as one of the leading sports writers in the country. Back in the early eighties, I actually appeared on a local talk show Povich hosted in Philadelphia and the man conducted a pretty fair interview, actually seeming to listen to what you were saying and responding appropriately.

But that was then. He's been doing *Maury* in various incarnations since 1991, and the show is the last word in—I'm searching for the right term—"tawdriness"? Yes, that'll certainly do. So will "exploitation." And "the lowest common denominator." My friend Bernie Goldberg, in his book *100 People Who Are Screwing Up America*, actually had Povich slotted at No. 31, ahead of such world-class creeps as Springer, Al Franken, Maxine Waters and David Duke. Bernie described Povich's show as a "cesspool" and opined that after watching *Maury* and *Jerry* back to back, as WPIX viewers have the opportunity to do each weekday morning, "there's not enough soap in all of North America to make you feel clean—ever again."

I'm afraid I'm responsible for that, since I turned Bernie on to Maury's unique brand of television. In fact, in his takedown of *Maury*, he quoted at length the piece I wrote on the *Maury* phenomenon after watching him, transfixed, as an escape from the agony of my back.

But here is where I disagree with Bernie: Where he sees unadulterated crap, I see crap that is immensely revealing and, yes, in its creepy way highly instructive.

For the chief feature of Povich's show, the element that has enabled it to thrive all these years, is young women—Hispanic, white, but most often black—seeking to determine the paternity of their children. One after another they troop onto Maury's stage, and (as the image of an adorable infant or toddler stashed backstage is projected to the ooohs and ahhhs of the studio audience) accuse some young guy of being the father. The accused then walks (or as often struts) on stage and denies paternity, which generally involves pointing to the kid in question, and emphasizing how dramatically the child's features differ from his own. He'll also often cast aspersions on the mother's character, peppering her with variations of the words "slut" and "whore." While the tenor of these encounters vary—sometimes the woman is tearful, more often angry; sometimes the guy is good humored or even likable—the basic formula is fixed. Presenting himself as an impartial arbiter, Maury oversees the frequently profanity-laced bouts of recriminatory mayhem and then, after a couple of minutes (they've surely done studies on the average viewer's attention span) tears open the manila envelope with the paternity tests and reads the results. "When it comes to two-year-old Jadiem, Corey, you *are* the father," or, just as often, "When it comes to 10-month-old Treasure, Earnell, you are *not* the father."

If the woman finds herself vindicated, she usually leaps to her feet, exultant, and berates the man. One mother I saw spun around, thrust her backside to the camera and, pointing, screamed at the newly established dad, "Kiss my ass!" When the man is victorious, he is likely to throw up his hands like a triumphant athlete, as the woman, bursting into tears, runs backstage, Maury trailing after her—both followed by a cameraman who records the host consoling her.

This human drama makes, I'm embarrassed to admit, for riveting television. For what we are witnessing is tragedy on a scale beyond anything else on the dial. Here are all the lamentable statistics made flesh, romance in black urban America in microcosm. The supply of accusers and accused seems inexhaustible. One mother I saw was back on Povich's stage for a fifth time, testing two men (the seventh and eighth she'd had tested overall) for paternity of her toddler Mustafa—neither proving a match, as it turned out.

But almost as telling is the attitude of Maury Povich himself as he surveys the human wreckage before him. As much a part of the routine as the placement of the chairs on the set, he makes an elaborate pretense of concern for the future well-being of his guests and their offspring, paying lip service in general terms to the doctrine of personal responsibility. If the DNA establishes a given man as a child's father, he always asks the guy if he now intends to become part of the child's life. Unfailingly comes the response: "Yeah, I'm a man, I'll step up to the plate." Or, "I'm a man, I take care of my business."

With the young women—or, actually, more often girls— he will be solicitous, almost paternal. "Sophia, let me ask you a question, because a lot of people are wondering this," he said gently to one young woman before the results were in. "You say you got pregnant with him once before and had a miscarriage, and you say he laughed at you. So why would you sleep with him again?"

It is likely that in some cases these few on-camera seconds with Maury are as close to actual fatherly commiseration they've ever experienced.

"You've got two children together," he said to one pair, screaming profanities at each other after the man's paternity has been established. "Don't you want them to grow up in a home where their mother and father respect each other? Don't you want that?"

Alas, watching the two of them stare back blankly, it seemed pretty clear that such a thought—*Respect each other?*—had never pierced the consciousness of either one; and that as soon as they left the studio, the guy would be out of the kids' life. Not that it would be much of a loss, given that he'd already been shown, by every standard by which men once measured themselves, to be utterly useless.

Which is to say, the problem is not so much that Povich's *pro forma*, Ad Council-approved advice dispensed to these two and so many others is *wrong*, exactly, it is just staggeringly, mind-blowingly insufficient. And pointless. And, like so much of the pap that gushes forth from such people, intended mainly to soothe his own conscience. What cries out to be said is the one thing no TV host who cares about staying on the air never would: WHAT KIND OF IDIOTS ARE YOU? FOR GOD'S SAKE, STOP HAVING BABIES!

Instead, like the other post-sixties elites Maury clings to the doctrine that no sin is greater than passing judgment. So the show naturally also ignores the larger issue in plain sight: the moral confusion of the world these people inhabit. In fact, the only nod to that world comes in the ads between segments. While some are pitches for job training—in air-conditioning or automotive repair, hairdressing or secretarial work—a high proportion are for sleazy ambulance-chasing law firms: "If you've been injured in an accident, tell the insurance company you mean business!" In short: advertising for an audience largely detached from the 9-to-5 work economy and always up for free money.

Needless to say, the one word almost never heard on *Maury* is the one that would do his guests the most good: marriage.

The saddest part is that it's not like any of this is news. It was back in 1965, before the problem was remotely as severe as it is today, that Daniel Patrick Moynihan famously warned of "the unraveling of the black family." In retrospect, his report was a beacon in the night. Rampant illegitimacy, as he wrote, inevitably gives rise to "a tangle of pathology," and he went on to enumerate the now familiar catalogue of disasters in waiting, from joblessness to criminality. Parents are absolutely essential, the report proclaimed, because they "shape their children's character and ability. By and large, adult conduct in society is learned as a child," and lacking the stable, two-parent homes that marriage brings, children learn disorganization and practice chaos. The report concluded that "at the heart of the deterioration of the fabric of Negro society is the deterioration of the Negro family. It is the fundamental source of the weakness of the Negro community at the present time."

Tragically, the reaction to the report also presaged what was to come. Though Moynihan was a liberal Democrat (albeit a free-thinking one), serving at the time in LBJ's Great Society administration, he was roundly eviscerated. As Kay Hymowitz observed in *City Journal*, the liberal reaction to the prophetic report was "a resounding cry of outrage [that] echoed throughout Washington and the civil rights movement. . . . Civil servants in the 'permanent government' at Health, Education, and Welfare [HEW] and at the Children's Bureau muttered about the report's 'subtle racism.' Academics picked apart its statistics. Black leaders like Congress of Racial Equality [CORE] director Floyd McKissick scolded that, rather than the family, '[i]t's the damn system that needs changing.' . . . Family instability is a 'peripheral issue,' warned Whitney Young, executive director of the National Urban League. 'The problem is discrimination.' The protest generating the most buzz came from William Ryan, a CORE activist, in *Savage Discovery: The*

Moynihan Report, published in the *Nation* and later reprinted in the NAACP's official publication. Ryan, though a psychologist, did not hear Moynihan's point that as the family goes, so go the children. He heard code for the archaic charge of black licentiousness. He described the report as a 'highly sophomoric treatment of illegitimacy' and insisted that whites' broader access to abortion, contraception, and adoption hid the fact that they were no less 'promiscuous' than blacks. Most memorably, he accused Moynihan of 'blaming the victim,' a phrase that would become the title of his 1971 book and the fear-inducing censor of future plain speaking about the ghetto's decay."

So the unraveling of the black family only accelerated. In 1965, the increase in black illegitimacy since 1950 had been from roughly 18 percent to 24 percent; yet 15 years hence, in 1980, fully half of black births were out of wedlock, with the figure heading steadily toward the nearly three quarters of today.

It is not coincidental that illegitimacy has also risen sharply among other ethnic groups during this period, if not at quite the same pace; for society's abandonment of moral standards for the underclass—worse, the reflex to cast condemnation of such destructive behavior as racist—has inevitably led to a general suspension of the stigma against illegitimacy. Not very long ago in the United States, giving birth to a "bastard," the cold-hearted term of general usage, was a source of such intense shame that respectable families would go to almost any lengths to hide such a tragedy from even their closest friends. Both Bobby Darin and Jack Nicholson, born to young unmarried women in the late thirties, were raised by their grandparents, each believing his mother was his sister. Thirty years later, a girl I knew in college, beautiful and brilliant, disappeared for a semester and on her return told everyone she'd been ill with

Crohn's disease, an excuse so exotic and plausible sounding no one questioned it; and it was only a couple of years later, via her closest friend, that I learned the truth.

Indeed, my wife still recalls her no-nonsense, Arkansas-born father's stern advice as she headed off to Berkeley in the fall of 1967: "Priscilla, I don't care what you do, just don't come home with a bastard."

Though in fact my father-in-law happened to be a rocket scientist, this was hardly rocket science: At the time, most middle-class fathers would've said a variation on the same thing. Judgmental? You're damn right. But that's before judgment—and, indeed, stern fathers—became suspect, and we were all better off for it.

Of course, the rise of the feminist movement in the sixties and seventies, with its relentless war on the alleged sins of patriarchy, played a monumental role in altering attitudes about not just illegitimacy but the very necessity of the nuclear family. When T-shirts bearing the cheeky slogan "A woman without a man is like a fish without a bicycle" first began appearing on braless young chests, who could have imagined it would come to this? Yet, so well-positioned were the movement's proponents at key crossroads of the culture—from academia, to media, to government—that within two generations they succeeded in eroding what had for millennia been basic human understandings: chief among them, that children need fathers.

It is a measure of how far we have descended that even an iconic conservative like Sarah Palin has been able to survive the pregnancy of her unmarried teenage daughter politically unscathed. In fact, she's turned it into a kind of virtue, opining that the experience has given her special insight into "the pain and challenges that accompany when your wonderful, smart, 'it-could-never-happen-to-her' 17-year-old daughter" and that Bristol is now "out there telling other girls 'don't do what

I did.'" Still, a couple of generations back such a thing happening in the home of a governor would have been all but inconceivable. And if Bristol *had* stupidly gotten herself knocked up by a lowlife like Levi Johnston, you can damn well bet that Todd Palin would have been at Johnston's door the night he learned of it with the proverbial shotgun.

Needless to say, the legions of purposeful and self-absorbed women at the feminist movement's core were cushioned from the consequences of what they preached. Overwhelming white, upper middle class and college educated, they and their children have been impacted only minimally by the sea change in cultural mores. Not so the lower classes, who had precious few other moorings to stability. As Moynihan presciently observed of America's fatherless inner cities nearly a half century ago, "a community that allows a large number of men to grow up in broken families, dominated by women, never acquiring any stable relationship to male authority, never acquiring rational expectations about the future—that community asks for and gets chaos."

Or as a contemporary politician, Indiana's Mike Pence, rightly observes of the current trend, "You would not be able to print enough money in a thousand years to pay for the government you would need if the traditional family continues to collapse."

For all that, we continue to see celebrities heedlessly casting the institution of marriage as outdated or pointless. "Women are realizing more and more that you don't have to settle, they don't have to fiddle with a man to have that child," said Jennifer Aniston in the summer of 2010, promoting her movie *The Switch*, in which she played a single mom impregnated by artificial insemination. "They are realizing if it's that time in their life and they want this part they can do it with or without that."

Given, the grasp of socioeconomic issues of Aniston and her fellow Hollywood narcissists is roughly akin to a fish's knowledge of a bicycle. But their powerful influence on the larger culture is undeniable. Spotting yet another *People* or *Us* piece glamorizing single motherhood, one can't but wonder: do editors at those places, or the *Access Hollywood* producer responsible for "Hollywood's Sexiest Single Moms," ever so much as pause to reflect on the consequences of such stuff? Are they really so clueless or indifferent as to not grasp that celebrating a choice by Jamie Lynn Spears or Nicole "Snooki" Polizzi to raise a child on her own might influence a confused 15-year-old girl in the South Bronx or Newark?

A thought experiment: As a change of pace, how about a *People* magazine cover—or, better yet, one of those especially stylish *Vanity Fair* covers shot by Annie Leibovitz—showing one of those famous single Hollywood moms locked in stocks, the way they used to do it in the Massachusetts Bay Colony, accompanying an article titled, without irony, "Shame! Shame!"

No, I wouldn't hold my breath, either.

Not that it's only the celebrity press that has amplified the destructive message that marriage is highly overrated. When the George W. Bush administration proposed a $1.5 billion initiative in support of marriage, the *New York Times* quickly ran a lead editorial vigorously denouncing it. "The whole idea of encouraging poor people to get married and stay married through classes and counseling sessions ignores the main reason that stable wedlock is rare in inner cities," it predictably declared, "the epidemics of joblessness and incarceration that have stripped those communities of what social scientists call 'marriageable' men."

Actually, the men who appear on *Maury* for paternity tests are often neither jobless nor criminally inclined. In fact, more than a few are clearly bright and even charming in a n'eer do well sort of way. Things being what they are, they just see no reason to get hitched, especially with no one pressuring them to do so. As one explained himself, with all the breezy confidence of Elizabeth Hurley's baby's daddy, billionaire producer Stephen Bing: "Any time I wanted a booty call, I'd call her. . . . She's the neighborhood 'ho.'" And, he added for good measure, "The baby does not look like me at all."

By now the chronic irresponsibility of young black men is such a given, it scarcely even arouses interest, let alone outrage. A few years back, a brief story from the *New Orleans Times-Picayune* on the death of a drug dealer made the Internet rounds, evoking much dark humor for its knee-slapping characterization of the dead man. "Larmondo 'Flair' Allen," it began, "an entrepreneur, died Feb. 7 of gunshot wounds on Martin Luther King Boulevard. He was 25." But the topper was the list of young Flair's survivors, including eight brothers, five sisters—and three sons and six daughters. Then, again, how different is his case in this regard from that of New York Jets star cornerback Antonio Cromartie, who by age 26 fathered nine children, in six states, by eight women?

Only once, briefly, was the country's focus squarely on the role of popular culture as cheerleader and enabler in the nation's calamitously high out of wedlock births; and even then, such a concern was dismissed as laughable by the free thinkers of the liberal elite. The butt of their jokes was, of course, Vice President Dan Quayle, whose "*Murphy Brown* speech," delivered on May 19, 1992, in San Francisco to the Commonwealth Club of California, came in the immediate aftermath of the devastating riots down the coast in L.A. following the Rodney King verdict. With much of L.A. still smoldering and 53 dead, his aim was to address the general "poverty of values" that underlay the violence. "When I have been asked during these last weeks who caused the riots and the killings in L.A., my answer has been direct and simple," Quayle said. "Who is to blame for the riots? The rioters are to blame."

In fact, the *Murphy Brown* reference was incidental. The vice president had never even seen the sitcom—the fatal line, "It doesn't help matters when primetime TV has *Murphy Brown*, a character who supposedly epitomizes today's intelligent, highly paid professional woman, mocking the importance of fathers by bearing a child alone and calling it just another lifestyle choice," was inserted by his speechwriter, Lisa Schiffren. So Quayle was genuinely taken aback by the firestorm it provoked.

First came the mockery—how this idiot who couldn't even spell potato was at it again, this time wasting everyone's time attacking a mere sitcom character. Left-of-center comedians had a field day. Typical was David Letterman, whose top 10 list the very next night—"Dan Quayle's top 10 other complaints about TV"—included:

"Not enough positive portrayals of really dumb guys."

"Too much liberal news coverage; not enough golf and cartoons."

"Practically have to be a brain surgeon to figure out how to turn it on and off."

Entertainment Weekly spoke for the entertainment/tabloid press in demanding: "Would Quayle be appeased if Murphy gave up her fatherless child to Major Dad, to be raised by a proper sitcom family?"

Not that those of the ostensibly serious media were any more thoughtful. At the time I was writing a column on TV and values for *TV Guide*, so I called my friend Goldberg, who was still at CBS, to ask how Quayle was playing in-house. His colleagues thought it was hilarious, Goldberg replied, almost to a man and woman dismissing out of hand the notion that Quayle was making a serious or reasonable point. And those outlets that did take Quayle at face value were almost uniformly hostile. Typical was the *Chicago Tribune*, which seized the occasion to editorialize on child poverty in America; repeating the leftist Children's Defense Fund's claim that "the number of American children living below the government's poverty level grew by more than 1 million" during the "Reagan-Bush boom years," even as it failed to note the blindingly apparent connection between child poverty and the very absence of fathers Quayle was addressing. Meanwhile, the *Los Angeles Times* editorial page explicitly endorsed *Murphy Brown* creator Diane English's view that "If the vice president thinks it's disgraceful for an unmarried woman to bear a child and if he believes that a woman cannot adequately raise a child without a father, then he'd better make sure abortion remains safe and legal"; and *Time* magazine approvingly quoted Hillary Clinton (whose husband was then seeking the Democratic presidential nomination), to the effect that Quayle was "typical of 'an Administration out of touch with America' and its growing ranks of single mothers." The *New York Times* sneeringly decried "the chill, abstract view of conservatives sure the true enemy is not poverty but poor people. . . . Remote from reality, he seems seriously to believe that what poor people most need is moral fiber. Make them work for their welfare, he says. Stop subsidizing broken families. That'll shock 'em into line."

Which is to say that ultimately the *Murphy Brown* brouhaha served less to highlight the poverty of values in America's inner cities than those that predominate in the country's newsrooms and leading universities.

In the face of the sustained assault, Quayle's resolve withered. That fall, in the midst of what would be a losing campaign against Bill Clinton and Al Gore, the Vice President watched the show in which *Murphy Brown* answered him back by name with a group of single mothers in an inner-city Washington apartment. Afterward, he stiffed upper lipped it to reporters on the street outside, insisting, "I was never criticizing single mothers."

True enough, less than a year later, in April 1993, the *Atlantic* ran a piece by Barbara Dafoe Whitehead titled, and indeed saying, "Dan Quayle Was Right," which generated much interest among thoughtful readers, and even favorable comment. But it made little impact upon the public or, more importantly, public policy. Indeed, nearly two decades later, when Mike Huckabee reprised Quayle—criticizing recent Oscar winner Natalie Portman for having a child out of wedlock, noting "there aren't really a lot of single moms out there who are making millions of dollars every year for being in a movie"—he so quickly found himself getting the Quayle treatment, he immediately backed off. His comments had been "distorted" by the "Hollywood media," he insisted, he wasn't criticizing Portman at all, let alone single mothers, so much as a society that enables them.

Sure, he was, and why not?

What's especially bizarre is that so many of the elite cultural arbiters moved and even horrified by the particulars of fatherless inner-city life in *fiction* seem utterly unable to draw the connection with what is happening every day a few miles from their offices. Many of the same people so ready to heap scorn on Quayle and Huckabee honor the aforementioned *Precious* as a masterpiece. A "rare blend of pure entertainment and dark social commentary," as the *Los Angeles Times* had it; "Too Powerful for Tears," (*Time*); "A glimpse inside a world we'd rather pretend does not exist in America," (*Huffington Post*); challenging "its audience's complacency as only a genuine work of art can" (the *New York Times*).

Complacency? The mind reels at their gall. Truly, these people are our own wretched version of F. Scott Fitzgerald's Tom and Daisy Buchanan, "careless people" who "smash up things and creatures and then retreat back into their money or their vast carelessness."

In the unlikely event they ever find themselves wondering how their views impact on actual flesh and blood human beings, they might try tuning in to *Maury*. Or, better yet, take a look at the piece my friend Gerry Garibaldi, an English teacher at an urban vocational-technical high school in Hartford, Connecticut., wrote for *City Journal*. It is a stunning front-line account of dealing with the pregnant girls in his classroom—and, unlike in fiction, there are no faux happy endings.

"Teen pregnancy, to the urban teacher, has become the intractable problem that we cannot teach our way out of," he writes. "Nearly all of my students are black or Hispanic. The vast majority of them come from single-parent households or foster homes. Some have done stints in shelters, group homes, or have been dumped with relatives. For many, this chaos has spanned multiple generations. . . . I've escorted girls whose water has just broken, on their trembling, wobbly legs to the front office, where it barely raises an eyebrow. In today's urban high school, there is no shame or social ostracism when a girl becomes pregnant. Other girls in school want to pat her stomach. Her friends throw showers where meager little gifts are given."

Among many other things, he writes of his first encounter with teen pregnancy, courtesy of a girl named Nicole: A "pretty 15-year-old, who wore rings on every finger, great looped earrings, and had a red pen with fluffy pink feathers and a heart that lit up when she wrote with it." One morning she fell asleep at her desk. This had happened before, but this time, when Gerry rapped his knuckles on her desk, she offered only a weary "Leave me alone, Mister, I feel sick," and a moment later threw up in a wastebasket. He had Nicole in two classes, one of them journalism, and he thought it might be useful—at least to some of the other girls—if she and another pregnant girl wrote a joint essay about their experiences. Gerry started them off with a simple question no one in the class had evidently ever considered before: "Do you think getting pregnant when you're a teenager is a good thing or a bad thing?" Reluctantly taking on the assignment, with his "persistent nudging, they begin to pull out the statistics for the children of single parents—from the FBI: 63 percent of all suicides are individuals from single-parent households; Center for Disease Control: 75 percent of adolescents in chemical dependency hospitals come from single parent households; the Children's Defense Fund: More than half of all youths incarcerated for criminal acts come from single parent households, and on and on."

But the numbers fail to make an impression on Nicole or any of the others. "Nobody gets married anymore, Mister," comes the nonchalant refrain, and the girls soon drop the assignment. In the end, despite Gerry's persistent efforts, Nicole fails both his classes. After she gives birth to a healthy boy, she returns to school the following year with "a photo album with hearts full of photos of her boy."

"On my way home at night," he wrote toward the end, "I often see my students in the projects that surround our school, pushing their strollers or hanging out on their stoops, when they should be home doing homework. . . . Teenage girls like Nicole qualify for a vast array of welfare benefits from the state and federal governments: medical coverage when they become pregnant (called "Healthy Start"); later, medical insurance for the family ("Husky"); child care ("Care 4 Kids"); Section 8 housing subsidies; the Supplemental Nutrition Assistance Program; cash assistance. If you need to get to an appointment, state-sponsored dial-a-ride is available. If that appointment is college-related, no sweat: education grants for single mothers are available, too. Nicole didn't have to worry about finishing the school year; the state sent a $35-an-hour tutor directly to her home halfway into her final trimester and for six weeks after the baby arrived."

As for the young fathers, they "strut, swear and swagger. There's a he-man thing to getting a girl pregnant, which marks you as an adult in the eyes of your equally unmoored peers. . . . A boy's interest in his child quickly vanishes. When I ask girls if the father is helping out with the baby, they shrug indifferently. 'I don't care if he does or not,' I've heard too often."

Gerry said his students often ask questions about *his* personal life, and the one he hears most often is: "'Do you have kids?' 'Two,' I say. The next question is always heartbreaking. 'Do they live with you?'"

LET'S PRETEND NO. 3
CRIME HAS NOTHING TO DO WITH RACE

Jesse Jackson has said many objectionable things in his extended time on the national stage, as well as a few outright indecent ones. But with the possible exception of his "Hymietown" slur of Jewish New Yorkers, surely the first thing he would take back if only he could was his excursion into truth telling at a meeting of his Operation Push on Nov. 27, 1993, in the unexpected presence of a reporter: "There is nothing more painful for me at this stage of my life than to walk down the street and hear footsteps and start to think about robbery and then look around and see it's somebody white and feel relieved."

Not that any sensible soul would expect him to feel otherwise; certainly not very many of the millions of peaceable black Americans who, as the potential victims of rampant black-on-black crime, feel exactly the same way. According to the Department of Justice, black males between ages 14 and 17 are 10 times likelier than white teens to commit murder, and fully 93 percent of those killed by young black predators are also black. In Jackson's hometown of Chicago, between 2003 and 2008 blacks accounted for 78 percent of all juvenile arrests, as opposed to 18 percent who were Hispanic, and 3.5 percent who were whites.

It is a little different in New York, where in 2009, blacks comprised 24 percent of the population, but were 58 percent of murder victims and 73 percent of shooting victims; and while both perpetrators and victims are disproportionately young gang bangers, most targets of muggers and rapists are also far more likely to be black. Indeed, New York Police Commissioner Ray Kelly has gone out of his way to sympathize with the vast law-abiding majority among the city's black working poor and middle class, noting "how disproportionately the African-American community has suffered."

"As a black man," conservative commentator E.W. Jackson Sr. sums up the lamentable bottom line, "I am far more wary of the real black criminal than the imagined white racist."

This might well come as news to those who rely for their information on the mainstream press, whose coverage of issues involving black criminality is even more cowardly and craven than in other respects. A couple of decades ago, for reasons of sensitivity, virtually all media dropped the long-standing policy of routinely identifying suspected (or even convicted) perpetrators by race, maintaining that such a syndrome serves to abet the sin of racial profiling. In this, not unexpectedly, they have found support in social science "research"; for example, a 2002 report by "a media studies expert" out of Penn State asserting "African-Americans are especially likely to be mistakenly identified for perpetrators of violent crimes." Many outlets, while not going all the way, adopted a policy of not including suspects' race or ethnicity except in those cases where there was enough other identifying detail available that race might clinch the deal.

The result has been news reports like this, from the AP, on a murder in suburban Maryland:

"New details are starting to emerge in the stabbing death of a teenager in Germantown.

"Investigators now say 18-year-old Ezekiel Oak Babendreier was killed during what might have been an attempted drug buy and robbery. . . . The suspect seen with the knife is described as about 5'10" tall and 160 pounds. He is believed to be between 18 and 22 years old. Police say he has cornrows and was wearing a black do-rag, a black tank top and blue jeans at the time of the incident.

"The second suspect is described as 5'4" and 160 to 170 pounds. He has short black hair."

And media conglomerates actually pay "experts" to determine why readers and viewers are losing faith in their ability to give them the straight dope! They'd do far better sitting down with Leigh Barratt, a reader (or former reader) of the *San Diego Union-Tribune* who was so disgusted by that paper's similar treatment of an armed break-in at a local residence that he sat down and dispatched the following to the reporter who wrote the story: "Why don't you say the race of these idiots? . . . If they are black, then write that they are black. Stop being so politically correct and report the news. Report who did it. How are people in that neighborhood and elsewhere in San Diego (to) know who to be on the lookout for? Four Asian guys, four white guys, four Hispanic guys? Get the point? Stop sanitizing our news and tell the truth to the people of San Diego about who is committing these crimes."

But, hey, it's not as if one generally has to read too deeply between the lines to figure it out. Take this one, from the *New*

York Post, on the city's first murder of 2011. The victim, "Dwayne Haughton, 29," was a "father of three and musician who tried to break up a fight outside a Queens banquet hall," resulting in a gunman pumping three bullets into him. Three paragraphs in we read: "'I saw the flash and heard three shots,' said witness Lloyd Pulley, who tried to save the victim with CPR. 'I saw him take his last breath.' Pulley, 35, told the *Post* that shortly before the gunfire, he saw Haughton and three women being followed by a fourth woman yelling: 'What's up, bitch? Wanna fight?'"

It was fairly safe to presume this woman was not a Park Avenue matron or, say, a recent immigrant from Bangladesh.

Still, even if the race of those involved is so clear as to have been declared in neon, why should such information not be straightforwardly included the story? Isn't the job to report the news fully and dispassionately, rather than to protect readers from the facts?

But, of course, who's kidding whom: It's not the facts that our betters in the media are looking to protect readers from, it's their own presumed prejudices.

Chicago Tribune columnist and editorial writer Steve Chapman came right out and said it. After bands of young thugs began attacking tourists on Michigan Avenue's normally safe Magnificent Mile in early June 2011—and the *Tribune* drew the ire of many readers by refusing to identify the assailants by race—Chapman lashed out in righteous indignation. "Here's my question about the teenagers who have been attacking and robbing people on North Michigan Avenue in recent days:" he began his astonishing piece. "Were they Christians? And if so, what denomination? Baptist? Catholic? Seventh Day Adventist?

"Those may sound like ridiculous questions. But so is the question raised by many *Tribune* readers about our coverage: Why aren't we mentioning that the culprits are black? . . .

"If a reporter goes out and interviews people about the weather, would it make sense for the story to say, 'Joe Smith, who is black, is hoping for a cool front'? If a pedestrian gets run over by a bicyclist, should the story mention that the rider was white?

"In the attack coverage, what difference does race make, unless police are putting out descriptions or sketches in hopes of getting tips from witnesses? . . .

"And what good would it do to trumpet the skin color of the thugs? So pedestrians on Michigan Avenue can run away when they see two or more African-Americans? . . .

"My question to readers accusing us of political correctness is: Why do you care so much about the attackers' race? If you fear or dislike blacks, I suppose it would confirm your prejudice. But otherwise, it tells you nothing useful."

Unsurprisingly, the column elicited a torrent of responses, some outraged or contemptuous, others merely bemused, but what they had in common was a command of basic common sense glaringly absent in Chapman's screed. "The idiocy evident in this absurd analogy," wrote one reader, of the *Tribune* man's comparison of the crime spree with a weather report, "ought to disqualify the author from commentary upon anything more serious than the weather." "What an incredibly naive article," another correspondent opined. "People want to know for the simple reason that the more information one has about perpetrators of crimes, one is better able to judge the relative safety one enjoys in a given situation." Mused someone else, "I wonder if gangs of teenage white lower middle-class males banded together, picked a black middle-class neighborhood, then traveled there as a group, got off and then went on a fast-paced series of violent attacks and robberies on terrified black people (plus a Japanese tourist) . . . would anyone be bringing up race?" Then there was the guy who simply came back with a dismissive "Yes, whether criminal behavior is expo-nentially more common among blacks is not a useful thing to know. Idiot."

This gets at the real problem here, the one that when it comes to the subject of race in America becomes almost tediously redundant: Where race is concerned, the progressive narrative is unchanging, and impervious to the facts on the ground. That so many of the inner-city young are seemingly conscienceless cannot possibly have to do with the values, or lack thereof, with which they were raised; nor could it have a thing to do with kids growing up in homes without fathers; no, it is a consequence of racism and poverty, lousy schools and (never mind the tens of billions of wasted dollars poured into the inner cities since the sixties) the indifference of the larger society. Indeed, talk of the failings of underclass culture is not just an ugly distraction, it is *itself* racist. As observes Heather Mac Donald, the nation's most unflinchingly brave reporter on issues surrounding race and crime, a program launched by Chicago's school superintendent to combat youth violence might have done some good if the youth advocates assigned to at-risk kids "provided their charges with opportunities to learn self-discipline and perseverance, fired their imaginations with manly virtues, and spoke to them about honesty, courtesy, and right and wrong." But instead, they "couldn't be more mired in the assiduously non-judgmental ethic of contemporary social work."

Of course, the claim of poverty as an excuse for criminality has a pedigree predating Jean Valjean and *Les Miserables*, and for the good hearted and soft headed it obviously has emotional appeal. But even cursory examination reveals it to be just as obviously bogus. As the conservative black economist Walter Williams notes: "From 1900 to 1929, the nation's murder rate rose from 1.2 per 100,000 of the population to 8.4. However, during parts of the 1930s, when the unemployment rate stood at 37 percent, the murder rate had fallen to 6.3 per 100,000 and to 4.7 per 100,000 by 1960. After 1960, violent crime rates shot up. By 1993, the murder rate was 9.5 per 100,000, falling to 8.2 in 1995. Rather than poverty causing crime, one might more easily make the case that crime causes poverty."

In fact, it was during the very period when the government was pouring more resources than ever into the inner cities that crime there reached epidemic proportions.

This is not to suggest that using the unhappy statistical realities of race and crime as a means of anticipating criminality—i.e., to profile—is anything like an easy issue. The very idea runs contrary to the color blindness which for many of us is not just an ideal, but the only route away from America's dispiriting fixation on race. It is also powerfully and understandably offensive to the innumerable decent souls, especially among the highly targeted young, who find themselves subject to special scrutiny owing to the color of their skin. I'll never forget how distressed and humiliated my daughter was when she went into a drugstore in our overwhelmingly white suburban town with a black friend, and the other kid was aware of being followed everywhere she went. In an ideal world such a thing would never happen.

But it's also true that one's attitudes toward criminality, like much else, tend to be based on real-world experience, and it's an excellent bet the guy in the store had some with black teens and theft. Is that racist? If so, then presumably so are the (black) proprietors of convenience stores in South Chicago, where everything from toothpaste to Q-tips is locked away behind heavy plastic.

Those liberals and black activists who make an issue of the rates of black surveillance, arrest and incarceration surely know this, yet seem never to factor it into their enlightened worldview. To the contrary, it is part of the mission of the prestige media to attack—which is to say, undercut—all crime-fighting measures that involve race.

In October 2010, for instance, the *New York Times* prominently featured a story headlined, with the usual subtlety the paper brings to this issue, "Study Finds Street Stops by N.Y. Police Unjustified." Based on the Center for Constitution Rights' analysis of NYPD data between 2005 and the first half of 2008, the *Times's* report was accusatory from word one: "Tens of thousands of times over six years, the police stopped and questioned people on New York City streets without the legal justification for doing so, a new study says.

"And in hundreds of thousands of more cases, city officers failed to include essential details on required police forms to show whether the stops were justified, according to the study written by Prof. Jeffrey A. Fagan of Columbia Law School.

"The study was conducted on behalf of the Center for Constitutional Rights, which is suing the New York Police Department for what the center says is a widespread pattern of unprovoked and unnecessary stops and racial profiling in the department's stop-question-and-frisk policy. The department denies the charges."

Damn right it does. For while a typically credulous *Times* reader is always ready to be outraged by police misconduct, especially if the alleged victims are minorities, the facts, those troublesome things, are on the cops' side. In 2009, for example, blacks, who comprised roughly 23 percent of the city's population, accounted for 55 percent of all stop-and-frisks, while whites, 35 percent of the population, accounted for just 10 percent of all stops—which certainly *sounds* bad. Until, that is, one factors in that during that same period blacks committed 66 percent of all violent crimes (including 80 percent of shootings) and whites committed 5 percent of all violent crimes;

which is to say, based on those rates of criminality, blacks were actually being *under*stopped and whites *over*stopped.

As Mac Donald cogently observes at the opening of her 2003 book, *Are Cops Racist? How the War Against the Police Harms Black Americans*, "[T]he anti-profiling crusade thrives on ignorance and a willful blindness to the demographics of crime."

Yet in the current atmosphere so pervasive is the idea that profiling is an absolute and indefensible evil that a sudden sighting of basic judgment qualifies as an event.

To be sure, there is perhaps an honest case to be made against racial profiling as a crime prevention measure. As noted, it can indeed be burdensome for ordinary citizens and, yes, a keen source of humiliation.

But that is not its purpose. Such measures are in place, where they are, because they work. They reduce crime—significantly—and help put bad people behind bars.

Nor, if the most vociferous foes of racial profiling are to be taken at face value, do they necessarily approve even of *that*. Who can forget that now classic howler of a *Times* headline, "Despite Drop in Crime, an Increase in Inmates?" Appearing Nov. 8, 2004, under the byline of veteran reporter Fox Butterfield, the piece dealt not just with the "paradox" of the link between locking criminals up and reduced crime, but raised the familiar complaint that the criminal justice system has ingrained bias against minorities, and young blacks in particular. Noting the disproportionate number of black men in prison—"44 percent of state and federal prisoners in 2003," compared with 35 percent who were white and including "almost 10 percent of all American black men ages 25 to 29"— it quotes at length criminologist Alfred Blumstein of Carnegie Mellon University on the "many ways" the "self-defeating" system gives blacks a raw deal.

Once again, the facts get in the way. According to the federal Bureau of Justice Statistics, the black incarceration rate mirrors almost exactly the rates of black criminality and arrest. To retrieve just the most telling number from a blizzard of data, blacks, comprising that shocking 44 percent of federal and state prisoners, committed a fraction over 52 percent of all the murders in the United States between 1976 and 2005.

Indeed, it is easy to make the opposite case that, far from being targeted for special abuse, overall blacks receive greater leniency in punishment. The indispensable Mac Donald points, for example, to "a 1994 Justice Department survey of felony cases from the country's 75 largest urban areas (that) discovered that blacks actually had a lower chance of prosecution following a felony than whites did and that they were less likely to be found guilty at trial." And while blacks were indeed more likely to receive prison sentences after conviction, such an outcome invariably reflects the gravity of their offenses and the fact of prior criminal records. This last has been confirmed by other studies, Mac Donald adds, including a number by avowedly liberal criminologists. For instance, Michael Tonry of the University of Minnesota Law School observes, "Racial differences in patterns of offending, not racial bias by police and other officials, are the principal reason that such greater proportions of blacks than whites are arrested, prosecuted, convicted and imprisoned."

Likewise, the "driving while black" charge falls victim to reasonable scrutiny. Such a charge was long aimed, for instance, at troopers on the New Jersey Turnpike, a notorious drug trafficking route—until a comprehensive study commissioned by the state attorney general showed that while blacks comprise 16 percent of the drivers on the turnpike, they make up a quarter of those who exceed the speed limit by more than 15 miles per hour; yet only 23 percent of those pulled over for speeding were black. If that was racial profiling, they were doing a damn lousy job of it.

Still, what matters almost as much as the truth is perception, and there is no question that within much of the black community cops and the American system of justice are regarded with deep distrust and hostility. This is a fact with which prosecutors trying minority defendants must often contend; which is why, speaking of racial profiling, smart attorneys representing black defendants will often seek minority juries, in the expectation that they are especially likely to ignore evidence of guilt.

Of course, the most notorious example remains the O.J. Simpson verdict, where DNA evidence set the odds that someone other than Simpson might have committed the gruesome double murder at 1 in 170 million; making the jury's not guilty verdict as deplorable as any miscarriage of justice ever countenanced by racist whites in the Jim Crow South.

But a more pedestrian example is perhaps even more telling. Usually jurors more committed to racial solidarity than to the evidence or their consciences have the good sense to at least keep it to themselves. But according to the *Washington Post*, when a black juror named in an Albany, New York, drug case named Leslie Davis refused to convict in the face of overwhelming evidence, he showed no such reticence, announcing "the white jurors, they didn't understand what the neighborhoods were like where the black defendants lived or the struggles they faced even to survive."

Then there was the sensational 1990 drug case in the same paper's own backyard, wherein Washington Mayor Marion Barry was acquitted on 13 of 14 counts, despite a videotape of the mayor smoking crack in a Washington hotel room. Afterward, the trial judge, Thomas Penfield Jackson, declared he'd "never seen a stronger government case."

Essentially, that jury followed the lead of notorious bigot Louis Farrakhan, who showed up at the trial with a dozen menacing supporters, and declared that the proceeding was "part of the double standard that black people have been under since we have been in this country," and demonstrated "the wickedness of the United States government and the lengths to which this government will go when it targets a black leader to be discredited."

Five years later, a former special assistant U.S. attorney in the District of Columbia named Paul Butler, a black man himself, wrote a piece for the *Yale Law Journal* describing how at the time he and other newcomers to the D.C. office "were informed that we would lose many of our cases, despite having persuaded a jury beyond a reasonable doubt that the defendant was guilty. We would lose because some black jurors would refuse to convict black defendants who they knew were guilty."

What's even more unsettling in Butler's account is that "some of my fellow African-American prosecutors hoped that the mayor would be acquitted . . . because they believed that the prosecution of Barry was racist"—and that Butler himself came to agree with that view. In fact, the essay then goes on to make the case for black jury nullification, arguing "the decision as to what kind of conduct by African-Americans ought to be punished is better made by African-Americans themselves, based on the costs and benefits to their community, than by the traditional criminal justice process, which is controlled by white lawmakers and white law enforcers."

That such a seemingly reasonable guy should echo a racist thug like Louis Farrakhan may seem as incomprehensible as it is appalling, but it is not as surprising as it should be. Rather, it is just more evidence of how pervasive is the victim mentality within the black community. Predicated as it is on the notion that blacks ought legitimately be held to different—lower—

standards, black jury nullification is nothing more than affirmative action in the courtroom. Like the more conventional version, it stresses above all the superficials of race and ethnicity, and so fundamentally undermines the ideal of evenhandedness. When it comes to race, conventional rules, even if they happen to be laws, simply do not apply.

The same attitude is perhaps even more apparent in the relationship between black people and the police. Like so much of the rest, black suspicion of law enforcement, rooted as it is in the unhappy past, is perhaps to a degree understandable; especially since there are still some racist cops out there. But given that those most brutalized by thugs in their own communities are often reluctant to cooperate with police, such hostility has long since reached the point of irrationality and self-destructiveness. The police files bulge with frustrating examples of cases that should have been readily solved but haven't been for lack of cooperation. If one is fishing for infuriating examples, none better fits the bill than that of a toddler named Vinyette Trudy Teague. Way back on the evening of June 25, 1983, Vinyette, aged a year and a half, a foot and a half tall and weighing 27 pounds, was playing on a seventh floor hallway in her home in a Chicago project. The following is from a notice issued by the Chicago Police Department soon thereafter: "An estimated fifty people were in the hallway at the time, including Teague's cousins, two aunts, her uncle and many neighbors. At 9:30 p.m., Teague's grandmother left her alone for a few minutes to answer a phone call. When she returned, the baby was gone. The police were called at 3:00 a.m., after Teague's parents returned home. Although the gallery was packed with people and there were only three exits, nobody saw anything suspicious. . . . If you have any information concerning this case, please contact: Chicago Police Department."

Nearly 30 years on, no one has come forth with any such information.

This is sheer insanity, but what's worse is that it is insanity that is actually *promoted*, notably in rap music. Little wonder that no arrest has ever been made in the rubouts of two of the most revered rappers of all time, Tupac Shakur in 1996 and his archrival Notorious B.I.G. a year later. "Snitches get stitches and wind up in ditches," as the mantra of big time New York rap station Hot 97 has it; never mind that one of its own personalities, a 32-year-old DJ who called himself Megatron, was killed in 2011 in an apparent mugging gone wrong.

What can be almost as baffling is the contempt and anger with which so many black people regard those in authority who've made it their policy to aggressively combat inner-city crime. In New York, for example, Rudy Giuliani continues to be derided as a mean-spirited racist for, among other things, having instituted a stop-and-frisk policy in the city's most crime-ravaged neighborhoods when he was mayor. In 1999, a rap group called Screwball went so far as to produce a song happily envisaging the mayor's murder.

Coincidentally, around the same time the song was making news, so were the latest crime statistics. They showed that as a result of Giuliani's policies New York's murder rate was in free fall, especially benefiting minority neighborhoods. In Harlem's 28th Precinct, between 1993 and 1998 murders plummeted 77 percent; in Bedford-Stuyvesant's 81st Precinct, they fell 62 percent. Someone did the math, and it was determined that had murders continued at the pre-Giuliani rate, 308 more whites would have died in those years, 1,842 Hispanics, and 2,299 blacks.

Of course, violent crime will always be a fact of urban life. Even in the current era of reduced crime that prevails in most inner cities today, the papers are full of tragic stories. That will not change.

But what can change, and must, if we are ever to fully bridge the racial divide in this country, are our expectations about the *nature* of criminality.

When, exactly, will that happen? When Jesse Jackson, along with the rest of us, can hear footsteps walking down a quiet street and, turning around to see a black kid, think nothing of it.

It was on Nov. 4, 1995—I know because later the same day Yitzhak Rabin was assassinated—that I chanced upon a radio interview with the brilliant conservative economist Thomas Sowell as I drove from our Westchester home to the Bronx to visit my Aunt Rose. Sowell was discussing Washington, D.C.'s historically black Dunbar High School, and it was riveting. Although I'm a history buff, and enjoy nothing more than poking around neglected corners of the country's past, the Dunbar story was entirely new to me. But what made Sowell's narrative so compelling—and enormously heartening—was that it suggested a clear path from the morass of educational underachievement that afflicts so many black kids today.

"In 1899, there were four academic public high schools in Washington, D.C.—one black and three white," Sowell subsequently observed in his book *Black Rednecks and White Liberals.* "In standardized tests given that year, students in the black high school averaged higher test scores than two of the three white high schools."

The contrast with today could hardly be more striking. There are many images that come to mind when reflecting on the state of inner-city schools in contemporary America. Metal detectors at school house doors. Uniformed cops in hallways. Classrooms so chaotic that maintaining basic order is a higher priority than teaching or learning. But of late, perhaps one edges out all the rest: the "changing parties" thrown by Atlanta teachers so they could have a good time as they scrupulously changed the scores of the overwhelmingly minority students on standardized tests, so as to pretend they were actually learning something. "Just imagine a young person, who was recently hired or accepted to college on the strength of one of those faked diplomas, receiving the rude awakening of a firing or college flunk-out all because he couldn't actually read or write," writes PJ Media's Kyle-Anne Shiver, a graduate of Atlanta's public school system in better days. "Thinking of all those lied-to kids and their disillusionment made me cry. It's hard to imagine adults in responsible positions—teachers, for crying out loud!—so callously hurting the children they were employed to help."

The Dunbar students of more than a century ago Sowell describes required no such sympathy, despite the all-too-evident handicap of living in a time when slavery was still a recent memory, recalled first-hand in innumerable black households in its odious particulars. Moreover, Sowell made clear that the school's remarkable success rate was not attributable to a policy of selective admissions to the school, since Dunbar welcomed all comers; in fact, the overwhelming majority of its students were from the very lowest echelons of society. "Over the entire 85-year history of academic success of this school," he writes, "from 1870 to 1955, most of its 12,000 graduates went on to higher education. This was very unusual for either black or white high school graduates during this era. Because these were low-income students, most went to a local free teachers college but significant numbers won scholarships to leading colleges and universities elsewhere. . . . When the late black educator Horace Mann Bond studied the backgrounds of blacks with Ph.D.s, he discovered that more of them had graduated from M Street-Dunbar than from any other black high school in the country."

The record is little short of stunning: professors, judges, military officers, and entrepreneurs by the score. "The first black man to graduate from Annapolis came from Dunbar. The first black enlisted man in the Army to rise to become a commissioned officer also came from the same institution. So did the first black woman to receive a Ph.D. from an American university. So did the first black full professor at a major American university (Allison Davis at the University of Chicago). So did the first black federal judge, the first black general, the first black Cabinet member, the first black senator elected since Reconstruction and, among other notables, the doctor who pioneered the use of blood plasma, historian Carter G. Woodson, author and poet Sterling Brown, and Duke Ellington, who studied music at Dunbar."

How did it come about? It wasn't a matter of money—like most every black school, Dunbar was massively underfunded, with a dilapidated physical plant, crowded classes and a dearth of classroom materials. And it certainly wasn't because Dunbar's students got any sort of head start at home; a mere couple of generations removed from a time when it was a crime to teach blacks to read in much of America, many of their parents were barely literate.

The answer was as simple as in practice, then and now, it is difficult to achieve: work, discipline, self-reliance. The administrators and teachers at the school were the polar opposite of those who seem to have been very nearly the norm in Atlanta; they had high expectations, both for their charges and themselves. Truancy and tardiness were simply not tolerated. Students were expected to be attentive in class and to conscientiously complete their assignments outside of it, and so they did.

Then there were their parents. Crucially, for the overwhelmingly number of students, there were *two*. And while they might not have been able to help with homework, especially if their kids took Greek or Latin on offer at the school, they understood the value of their children's education to their futures.

While Sowell as always relies primarily on facts and data to make his case, he speaks also from personal experience. He writes that the schools he himself attended in 1940s Harlem were "ordinary urban ghetto schools," but there, too, the environment was infinitely more conducive to serious study than comparable schools are today, enabling him and others to blossom intellectually.

The formula is of course replicable today, as has been repeatedly demonstrated. Perhaps no modern educator has done so as dramatically, and over such an extended period of time, as the legendary Marva Collins. In 1975, after 14 years as a Chicago public school teacher, unhappy both with the quality of public education and with that her two youngest children were getting at private schools, Collins used $5,000 from her school pension fund to open the private Westside Preparatory School (now Marva Collins Prep) in Chicago's inner-city Garfield Park neighborhood. First setting up shop in her home with a class of six, including her own two, she relocated to a former warehouse, charging those parents who could pay $80 a month, and soon developed a reputation as an educational miracle worker. Under her tutelage, inner-city kids were reading fluently by age four, and older kids once deemed uneducable were soaring several grade levels above the national average in reading and math. By 1980, the school had 200 students (paying the now $200 tuition) and a long waiting list.

Her methods were the traditional ones—the same ones that had worked at Dunbar—but tradition having gone out of fashion, they seemed revolutionary. She was tough, demanding hard work and refusing to buy excuses. She insisted on proper grammar and elocution. She taught the classics—her second-graders read Shakespeare and by third grade, the kids were exposed to Aristotle and the Socratic method. "People ask me, 'How do you get the children to memorize *The Canterbury Tales* in Old English?'" Collins told a reporter. "I say, 'It never dawned on me that they couldn't learn it.'"

Her oft-repeated axioms were to the point: "Determination and perseverance move the world; thinking that others will do it for you is a sure way to fail." And "Excellence is not an act but a habit."

To white, middle-class (and overwhelmingly liberal) journalists this was catnip, the sort of feel good inner-city story they kill for. Little wonder that in 1979 Collins was the subject of an adoring *60 Minutes* profile. Before a startled Morley Safer, her first-graders volunteered Chaucer, Dante and Shakespeare as their favorite authors; and later, walking with the reporter through a neighborhood that looked more like a war zone, she vented a frustration millions of viewers surely shared. "All the money that's been thrown away, and not a doggone thing has changed in this area in the last 17 years," she said, indicating the teens lounging on the stoops of graffiti-marred buildings. "They couldn't read when we moved here, they can't read now. They didn't have jobs then, they don't have jobs now."

Little wonder that a couple of years later she was played by Cicely Tyson in a Hallmark Hall of Fame movie, with Morgan

Freeman co-starring as her husband. Or that she followed that with several best-selling books.

But her liberal fans eventually became aware that Collins came with some difficult baggage. Her methods were not just unconventional, to many in the entrenched educational establishment, they were threatening. Independent, opinionated and stubborn, she made no secret of her impatience with the teaching philosophies espoused by today's schools of education, which tend to cast the teacher as "facilitator" rather than (God forbid) rigorous authority figure, and with their abandonment of traditional phonics for "whole language," which encourages early learners to focus on meaning rather than actual reading and spelling. As she tartly observed, kids, and especially inner-city kids, have "to learn intensive phonics, all the regular and irregular sound patterns in the English language, not some bootleg version for sounding out the first and last letters of a word. I saw that if a child knew the rules for vowel and consonant sounds and for syllabification, and the exceptions to the rules, then that child could pick up anything and read it." Nor, needless to say, did she have much more use for teachers unions, for whom the needs of children are so often a distant second to the priorities of the membership.

These are the sorts of things reporters don't like to hear, let alone appear to endorse. So it is hardly surprising that we've heard so little from Marva Collins in recent years. "I said no," as she observed in March 2010, recalling the several times she was approached in her heyday about serving as Secretary of Education. "I've never taken any federal money, because I didn't want somebody else telling me which child could learn and which child couldn't." Worse, she said it to the graduates of a fundamentalist Christian school in rural Tennessee.

Collins dismisses out of hand the notion that any child cannot learn—the entirety of her own history testifies to the contrary. Still, she is characteristically blunt about the special ways in which black children are handicapped. Asked in a 2009 interview about how to begin turning around chronically low academic performances of inner-city kids, she went immediately to the crippling effects of low expectations. Like it or not, she said, young black kids tend to be evaluated on "the way they dress, the way they speak. We all have an image. It's the image people have of inner-city schoolchildren. I wanted to be certain that my children did not accept that image."

So frank an acknowledgement of the cultural burdens that must be overcome for inner-city black kids to succeed, in the classroom and elsewhere, is something else that has not endeared her to many of her onetime admirers. Liberals instinctively rise up with adamant indignation at such a claim, seeing it as the worst kind of cultural stereotyping. But even if they are loathe to admit it, many of them know that broad assumptions about cultural background and attitudes toward education are grounded in reality. Does anyone doubt that Tiger Mom Amy Chua's "tough immigrant way," as she calls it, has everything to do with the academic excellence of Chinese-American children like her own; or that, as she also observes, the children of immigrant "parents from Pakistan, India, Nigeria, Korea, Jamaica, Haiti, Iran, Ireland" are usually similarly motivated in the classroom.

Indeed, among the most impressive kids in my son's class at his New York City private school was a Jamaica-born girl living in the South Bronx. An academic and athletic superstar, as well as former grade president, when she got a full ride to Stanford—after turning down similar offers from Harvard and Yale—no one would have dreamed suggesting it had anything to do with affirmative action.

But inner-city culture rarely gives rise to that kind of ambition, or to the work ethic essential to see it realized. The numbers—14 percent proficiency among African-American eighth-graders in reading, according to the 2009 National Assessment of Education, and 12 percent in math; a barely 50 percent high school graduation rate—are likely only the prelude to the larger tragedy. As George Will grimly chronicles, citing research by the global management consulting firm McKinsey & Company, the achievement gaps between white and minority students portend nothing less than "the economic equivalent of a permanent national recession."

Meanwhile, from the Kaiser Family Foundation comes a report revealing that black kids spend more than 41 hours a week watching TV, as compared with 25 hours by their (hardly industrious) white peers. Unsurprisingly, the study once again demonstrates a clear link between excessive TV watching and poor academic performance. Among the heaviest "media users" (which takes into account video games and social-networking sites, as well as TV), lousy grades are not an occasional thing, but the norm; and with ever-increasing media options at young fingertips, things are only getting worse.

Academic studies of black underperformance tend to be only slightly less ominous. "Current trends in the academic performance of African American adolescents are an area of concern among educators," as the introduction to the article "The Relationship of Gender and Achievement to Future Outlook Among African American Adolescents" gingerly puts it. "Recent studies suggest that African American adolescents are at heightened risk for remedial instruction, school suspension, course failure, and school drop-out. Factors identified as contributing to limited academic performance among these youths include academic tracking, limited teacher support, cultural mistrust, and disidentification with the academic culture of school."

There are many, many such impressively titled studies, most simply giving a scholarly spin to the all-too-obvious. The National Science Foundation, for instance, weighed in with one that discovered "Black students have been found to possess more negative attitudes toward mathematics than have White students." Then there was one called "Perceptions and Attitudes of Black Students Toward School, Achievement, and Other Educational Variables," the aim of which was to compare "the perceptions and attitudes of gifted Black early adolescents (n=48) toward school, achievement, and other educational variables with Black students in a regular education (n=50) and potentially gifted program (n=50). Results indicate that gifted Black students held significantly different attitudes and perceptions than both potentially gifted students and regular education students relative to principles of the achievement ideology, attitudes toward school, attitudes toward academically successful students, and perceptions of parental achievement orientation."

File all of the above under the category "Duh."

And we haven't even touched on the matter of discipline— i.e., the fact that for teachers in many urban classrooms teaching runs a distant second to maintaining some semblance of order. Indeed, ethnic sensibilities being what they are, and regulations having increasingly swung the balance of power away from teachers and administrators, even the most disruptive and abusive kids know that the rules, such as they are, are effectively unenforceable. "President Barack Obama has joined the chorus of those deploring bullying," Thomas Sowell wrote in a 2011 column. "But his own administration is pushing the notion that a disproportionate number of suspensions or other punishments for members of particular racial or ethnic groups is discriminatory. In other words, if a school suspends more black males than Asian females, that is taken as a sign of discrimination. No one in his right mind really believes that, but it is part of the grand make-believe that pervades our politics and even our courts.

"For years," he continues, "there have been stories in New York and Philadelphia newspapers about black kids beating up Asian classmates. But do not expect anybody to do anything that is likely to put a stop to it. If these were white kids beating up Hispanic kids, cries of outrage would ring out across the land from the media, the politicians, the churches and civic groups. But it is not politically correct to make a fuss when black kids beat up Asian kids."

Little wonder that the most discouraging of the studies are those charting parental involvement—or, more often, the lack thereof—in their kids' academic lives. Those with the greatest emotional resonance include case studies of specific kids, like the one titled "The Role of Family in Future Outlook." On the bright side, it describes "Kim, a higher achieving girl" whose "goal was to become a forensic psychologist." Her parents (and, significantly, there were two of them) "like what I want to be and they are the ones who encourage me to want to go to college and do well in school. They want me to do really well in high school, go to college, do really well, get a good job, and then I can help them with retirement." Here the researcher makes notes that Kim smiles before continuing. "They want to make sure I get a scholarship for college, so that's what they are working on, but they think I am going to get one; they think I am a good student."

In stark contrast, and far more prevalent, are the "lower achieving" students. For instance, there's "Debra, a lower achieving girl, stated: I really don't talk to my mother. We don't talk about my report cards or nothing. When it [report card] gets there, my mother keeps it. I don't even see it—my mother keeps it and I don't talk about it and she don't say nothing." There's also "Jeremy, a lower achieving boy. . . . Jeremy noted minimal interactions with his family: 'I don't really talk to my mother that much—she comes home she is tired. She's on the phones all day, typing and running around and she be too tired. Unless she wants something out of the kitchen or someone to fix her a plate or something, I don't talk to her.'"

What none of the studies I ran across accounts for is something else that is key, but also unmentionable: the victim mentality pervasive among young blacks of all classes today. Fed by a multicultural agenda that stresses the importance of specifically black as opposed to common American experience, even within that narrow spectrum it is a drumbeat of grievance. Black history has been overlooked and undervalued by the mainstream culture, so goes the underlying assumption, and so has black literature, and everything else of particular "relevance"—that all-purpose, end-all-arguments word—to "people of color." And the impact on even some of the potentially best black students has been devastating.

More than in any report, insight into this vital subject is to be found in the pages of John McWhorter's brave and highly cogent *Losing the Race*, in which he writes of his differing experiences with black and white students while teaching linguistics at Berkeley. McWhorter reports that in his experience the "intersection between 'black American' and poor schoolwork is *not* idiosyncratic. . . . I have encountered this problem to some extent in *most* black students, class after class, year after year."

He offers innumerable examples of underperformance by his black students, from slapdash work and ignored assignments to disinterest in class and flat-out surrender in the face of difficulty, to excuses so lame that "the dog ate my homework" seems persuasive in comparison. Moreover, he goes out of his way to stress that those he dealt with at Berkeley were not inner-city kids, but "are almost all upwardly mobile, bright-eyed young people, many with cars, none of whom would be uncomfortable in a nice restaurant and many of whom probably do know which wine goes with chicken." The problem, it became clear, was that "The black Cult of Anti-intellectualism cast top scholarly achievement as treachery—and not just in 'struggling neighborhoods,' but even at the best public university in California."

Quite simply, concludes McWhorter—who understands how potentially dangerous such a forthright view is, even for a black man—"these students belong to a culture infected with an anti-intellectual strain, which subtly but decisively teaches them from birth not to embrace schoolwork too wholeheartedly."

Of course, the students themselves don't see it that way. In the grip of the victim mindset—despite overwhelmingly being beneficiaries of racial preferences and other programs guaranteeing them special consideration—they regard whatever problems they experience at school as just another manifestation of racism. Indeed, observes McWhorter, so pointedly do they see themselves as "black" rather than as "students" that many show little interest in *any* subject, academic or otherwise, unless it is tied directly to personal experience.

He writes of teaching two classes in the same subject, the history of black musical theater, in which the differences in attitude between black and white students were glaringly apparent. In a kind of inadvertent controlled experiment, the first class happened to be composed of predominantly white students, and though the material had nothing to with themselves or their biological forebears, they were actively engaged with it from the outset, regarding it as part of our rich common past. In contrast, McWhorter writes, in the second class, overwhelmingly made up of black students, "I might as well have been reading out of the phone book"—this, despite the fact he was dealing with *black* history. Indeed, the students perked up only "when I talked about discrimination people had encountered—they were open to being reinforced in Victimologist ideology." Then, and again when he reached the near-present and material with which the students were already personally familiar.

Oddly enough, I had a small taste of the same thing under very different circumstances several years back with a group of tough inner-city kids consigned for various criminal infractions to a group home in my suburban New York town. I'd volunteered to help those with a literary bent launch a newspaper, a project that quickly fell apart for lack of follow through on the part of everyone from the would-be editor in chief on down. But that aside, we all got on well, and at one point I decided to take four or five of the boys to an outing at Shea Stadium. En route, the kid in the front seat, urged on by the others, kept turning on the radio full blast to rap, and I kept turning it off, trying to get a conversation going. At last I tried telling them stories out of history, my favorite kind—but that wasn't working, either, until I finally hit on one that grabbed their interest. It was about the Lincoln assassination. It was the details that got them—how Booth planned the job, the way he sneaked up behind the president, the kind of gun he used and the particulars of his getaway—because they were more or less able to relate it to experiences of their own.

Still, at least it was genuine history, as opposed to the version too many educrats and administrators foist on minority kids these days in the interest of making it "relevant." In 2010, to cite an especially egregious example, the Oklahoma City school district produced a "hip-hop curriculum" for at-risk minority kids called Flocabulary that labeled the Founders "old dead white men" and otherwise reduced the nation's past to sub-MTV rating levels. "White men getting richer than Enron," goes a characteristic verse on James Monroe. "They stepping on Indians, women and blacks. Era of Good Feeling doesn't come with the facts."

It belabors the point to observe that rather than fostering a sense of shared heritage, such an approach breeds only contempt for America's sometimes troubled but generally glorious past. Little wonder that so many of today's young, of all backgrounds and ethnicities, view George Washington and Thomas Jefferson primarily as slaveholding hypocrites.

Like so much else wrong with modern America, the drive to present American history, especially to minorities, as a relentless tale of oppressors and oppressed—i.e., to promote multiculturalism by making the material more "accessible" and "socially relevant"—is directly traceable to the sixties. "The proponents of the black studies movement of the 1960s and 1970s argued that educational institutions in American society (with an emphasis on, but not exclusive to, the university) had to be radically transformed for humanity's sake," as Tufts black studies professor Peniel E. Joseph writes approvingly in the *Journal of African American History*. "Historically, black studies advocates supported the utilization of scholarship for the larger pursuit of social justice and a broader, more inclusive democracy. However, the 'modern black studies movement' represented perhaps the greatest political and pedagogical opportunity to fundamentally alter power relations in American society."

The aim, in brief, was to harness history to ideological ends and, not incidentally, turn it into therapy. While it's hard to know where this reached its most ludicrous heights, it may well be in the proposition, much in vogue among Afrocentric "scholars," that the Greeks lifted their philosophy from "black" Egyptians. Mary Lefkowitz, a professor of classics at

Wellesley, got so tired of getting called a racist for challenging this patent absurdity that she wrote an entire book referencing the rich historical record to clearly demonstrate why it was not so. But, then, Lefkowitz was relying on facts and, as she writes, for her opponents the facts were irrelevant, since the point was that students be "indoctrinated along party lines" and the fiction about the Egyptians "empowers black people to reclaim their rightful place as equal players in contemporary society." That, as she noted, the promotion of errant nonsense as legitimate history actually does young blacks a tremendous disservice, keeping "them from learning what all other ethnic groups must learn," is for these ideologues apparently of no concern.

Nor are many of today's diversity-obsessed English departments much better, with curricula at all levels having replaced writers of the classics with pipsqueaks, if not outright mediocrities, as long as they have the right skin tone, gender or sexual orientation; a trend which has implicated whole generations of students in what amounts to intellectual fraud. "The thing I like best about being a conservative is that I don't have to lie," as the novelist and screenplay writer Andrew Klavan so aptly put it. "I don't have to pretend that men and women are the same. I don't have to declare that failed or oppressive cultures are as good as mine. I don't have to say that everyone's special or that the rich cause poverty or that all religions are a path to God. I don't have to claim that a bad writer like Alice Walker is a good one or that a good writer like Toni Morrison is a great one."

"I refuse to double-check an author's sex and skin color for political correctness before opening up a book," echoed a letter writer to the *Los Angeles Times* named Neal McCabe, in response to an attack on traditional standards in that paper. "The *Adventures of Huckleberry Finn* is still the great American novel—no matter Mark Twain's whiteness or maleness or deadness—because Huck looks past the cultural doctrines of his place and time to see into the human heart."

Of course, this was before a professor of English, Auburn's Alan Gribben, decided that, never mind the human heart, the Twain classic's repeated use of the n-word was offensive to black sensibilities, and so needed editing, and he found a publisher to convert all 219 uses of the offending word to "slave."

This was too much even for many progressives, who were not only offended on free speech grounds but correctly argued that such a ham-handed change actually muted the book's powerful anti-racist message. Roger Ebert, for example, on hearing the news, instantly shot off a tweet to his more than three hundred thousand followers: "I'd rather be called a N***** than a Slave."

Then, again, it's what happened next that's far more telling. Ebert apparently believed that since he's a well-known progressive and married to a black woman he had immunity. But no such luck; instantly black people were bitterly renouncing his inaptly phrased but correct-on-substance tweet with tweets of their own. "Fair point," mocked the one that seemed to cut him most directly to the quick, "from some who's likely to be called neither." In response, Ebert caved, sending out a mass *mea culpa*: "You know, this is very true. I'll never be called a N***** *or* a Slave, so I should have shut the **** up."

If there's a lesson there, it's one that's already been long since proven: Driven by a toxic mix of condescension, paternalism and terror of giving offense, white liberals will almost *never* cross blacks claiming victimhood.

Still, the disastrous level of black educational underachievement is now so widely recognized, and poses so clear a threat to the nation's well-being, that the need to address it has resonated across the political spectrum. Issues like school vouchers, the utility of charter schools, even the need to curb the influence of teachers unions, once solely the province of conservatives, have been taken up by thoughtful progressives, too. Indeed, 2010 produced no fewer than three major documentary films on the appalling state of inner-city education, the most widely heralded of which, the heartbreaking *Waiting for Superman*, was directed by Davis Guggenheim, who won 2007's Best Documentary Oscar for Al Gore's environmental agitprop film, *An Inconvenient Truth*. (Unsurprisingly, given Hollywood's politics, this time his film wasn't even nominated.)

Around the country innumerable new schools focusing on the special needs of inner-city children have opened their doors over the past decade, many of them explicitly reflecting the methods and values that proved so successful at Dunbar a century ago and replicated by Marva Collins. Job one at such places is discipline, since inner-city life—and inner-city schools in particular—tend to be wracked by chaos. The mission statement of the Andre Agassi College Preparatory Academy, for instance, a charter school founded by the tennis star for at-risk minority kids in inner-city West Las Vegas, emphasizes "a child's character, respect, motivation and self-discipline." Its curriculum likewise makes no concessions to contemporary sensibilities, among other things stressing the classics.

Across the country in New York, the Harlem Village Academies charters also emphasize "character, behavior and habits of scholarship. Every student is expected to arrive on time every day, wear a school uniform, and follow a strict code of conduct. We make clear to our students from the beginning that we do not tolerate late homework, disrespectful words or even gestures, or any other 'minor' infractions."

Then there's the nine-school Success Charter Network, founded by former New York City Councilwoman Eva Moskowitz, archenemy of the city's teachers union, where children as young as four are drilled in walking silently through the halls and otherwise instructed in self-discipline. Here, if a child is late to school even once, both parent and child must report to school for a Saturday session. Third-graders at the first school in the network, the Harlem Success Academy, founded in 2006, are already scoring in the top one percent of New York's 3,500 schools in both reading and math. In a *Village Voice* profile, Moskowitz makes a point of the contrast between the library-like silence in her school and the "cacophony" that's the norm in the one with which it shares a building. "They're watching movies," she observes of the kids marooned in the other place. "Meanwhile, our kids are reading."

Though the educators behind such schools certainly never put it so baldly, all have consciously taken it upon themselves to address the glaring behavioral and character deficiencies so sadly evident in the communities—and, in many cases, the homes—into which their students were born. This is why in every case the parents are obliged to become partners in their children's education, with many requiring that they sign contracts committing them to take responsibility for both the behavior and academic performance of their offspring. "We reach out to build close relationships with parents and we offer guidance and suggestions for at-home strategies they can use to support their child's academic success," as Harlem Village Academies has it. "Teachers check in frequently to give progress reports, solicit feedback, and address concerns. We also create opportunities for families to build genuine relationships with one another through our potluck dinners, social events and activities. We survey our families regularly, asking for their feedback and ideas—and we follow-up on those ideas!"

Yet the melancholy truth, as any inner-city school teacher will tell you, is that for all the many black parents willing to commit such time and energy to their kids' academic well-being, systematically overseeing homework and meeting with teachers, innumerable others are so angry and defensive they take umbrage at the suggestion that they should. As former Florida Governor Jeb Bush observed in the *Wall Street Journal* of the fierce opposition he faced in trying to end social promotion in that state of eight- and nine-year-olds unable to read, "Holding back illiterate students seemed to generate a far greater outcry than did the disturbing reality that more than 25 percent of students couldn't read by the time they entered fourth grade."

Especially discouraging in this regard was the experience of Michelle Rhee, the fire-breathing school reformer hired to turn around the woeful, overwhelmingly black Washington, D.C. public school system. Backed by the mayor who appointed her, the intrepid Adrian Fenty, Rhee fought the teachers union to a standstill and set about firing provably ineffective teachers—most of them black—and making other long overdue changes. The result? Fenty received more than 70 percent of the white vote in his bid for reelection against a hack go-along-to-get-along black pol, and less than 20 percent of the black vote, and Rhee and her policies were tossed out with him. It is also notable that while conservatives were rightly appalled by this turn of events, prominent liberals rushed to give black D.C. voters cover. Rhee had attacked the school system "with an unseemly ferocity and seemed to take great delight in doing it," as then-*New York Times* columnist Bob Herbert actually managed to write, and "concerns raised by parents about Ms. Rhee's take-no-prisoners approach were ignored. It was disrespectful."

Not that there aren't signs of genuine progress out there in this regard, proverbial stalks of green poking through the snow. Back in 1988, for example, Marva Collins and a group of her Chicago-trained teachers were set to open a school in the Los Angeles community of Compton, but plans had to be dropped when the overwhelmingly black and Hispanic residents refused to join a local developer and outside donors in supporting the plan. Yet 22 years later, in 2010, with the deterioration of its schools having continued apace, Compton became the first district in the state to take advantage of a "parent trigger" reform law empowering parents at chronically failing schools, if able to command a majority, to turn them into charters At one especially lousy school, McKinley Elementary, more than 60 percent of the parents joined in seeking to toss out the administration; only to be met with fierce opposition—and naked intimidation—from the powerful California Federation of Teachers, whose president termed the reform "a lynch mob provision." The parents are still fighting for what they need and deserve.

If only they'd stuck with Marva Collins in the first place! By way of contrast, one school around the same time that did, the Milwaukee College Preparatory School, today turns out so many successful graduates it is known as the Miracle on 36th Street. Its founder, a Wisconsin investment manager named Ron Sadoff, even channels Collins, boasting that the school's kindergartners "begin to read by spring, and our third-graders can read Shakespeare and Dickens."

In fact, the school owes its existence to a report that Sadoff happened to catch on Collins and her methods on *60 Minutes*; not the original piece, but a 1996 follow-up. It was prompted by persistent charges from the Chicago teachers union and others with a vested interest in the status quo that Collins rigged the numbers to make her school look far more effective than it was. So *60 Minutes* set out to discover what had become of the precocious seven-year-olds they'd interviewed in the original broadcast 17 years before.

They tracked down 33 of the 34 former Bard-spouting first- and second-graders, who were now in their early 20s. Every one not in graduate school was working in a responsible job, a high percentage as teachers or police officers. *60 Minutes* had a statistician compare these outcomes with others of the same background who'd attended more typical inner-city Chicago schools at the same time and it was determined that five of the young people in the other school would be on welfare; one would be in prison; and one would have been murdered.

This was impressive indeed, a stunning testament to a remarkable teacher and her ways. But there were others who'd helped make it happen who went unmentioned in the second piece, though several had appeared in the original: the parents. As poor as everyone else in the neighborhood, they'd sought out Collins when her school was just starting, and managed to scrape together the $80 a month to get their kids out of the hellish local schools to which they'd been consigned. One mother told *60 Minutes'* Morley Safer that at her daughter's former school, she'd been informed that her child would never learn to read and she might be retarded. Another said she'd met with teachers and administrators at her child's old school "two and three times a week, because I was so concerned about him. He never wanted to study." If you retrieve the broadcast on YouTube, you can see how she paused at this point in the telling to smile, seeming hardly to believe how things had changed. "Every night now, when he goes to bed, I've got to take a book away."

LET'S PRETEND NO. 5
"ACTING WHITE" IS A PROBLEM (NOT THE SOLUTION)

Those with a taste for low political comedy will recall that two of America's most celebrated inadvertent practitioners of the form made almost precisely same gaffe at almost precisely the same time. The subject was then-Senator and incipient presidential candidate Barack Obama and his broad electoral appeal. First up was Joe Biden, in an interview with the *New York Observer* in late January 2007. Obama, enthused his future vice president, was "the first mainstream African American (presidential candidate) who is articulate and bright and clean and a nice-looking guy. I mean, that's a storybook, man."

Harry Reid—whose observation would not be revealed until the publication of the post-election best seller *Game Change*—was almost as upbeat about the young senator's chances, noting approvingly that the "light-skinned" Obama didn't have a "Negro dialect, unless he wanted to have one."

While both remarks were meant positively, each caused a firestorm and quickly elicited a craven apology. "I want to say that I truly regret that the words I spoke offended people I admire very much," offered Biden, adding that those who knew him understood they did not reflect "my history and my heart." Intoned Reid at a hastily called press conference: "I deeply regret using such a poor choice of words. I sincerely apologize for offending any and all Americans, especially African Americans for my improper comments."

That the remarks were indeed "offensive" and "inappropriate" was everywhere accepted as a given. After all, didn't they elicit condemnation from all the usual quarters? Eugene Robinson, *Washington Post*'s resident arbiter of all matters racial, declared himself particularly upset by Biden's "articulate" reference. For the typical black person, he wrote, it is "a word that's like fingernails on a blackboard. . . . Articulate is really a shorthand way of describing a black person who isn't too black, or, rather, who comports with white America's notion of how a black person should come across."

Reid had it a bit easier, since at the time he was facing a tough reelection campaign back in Nevada and liberals didn't want to add to his troubles. But Republicans, often equally ready to play the race card when it suits their purposes, rushed to the attack. National GOP Chairman Michael Steele was especially shameless, responding to Reid's comments by comparing them to former-GOP Republican Leader Trent Lott's 2002 praise of Strom Thurmond's segregationist past that cost him his job and claiming a double standard. "It's either racist or it's not," he proclaimed, insisting that Reid too should be forced to surrender his leadership post.

This was unadulterated hogwash. In fondly recalling Thurmond's former commitment to rigid segregation, Lott seemed to be praising behavior repellent to every decent

American's notions of fairness and equal justice. Reid's mistake, like Biden's, was a classic instance of what Michael Kinsley famously defined as a Washington "gaffe"—a politician inadvertently telling the truth.

It was not even an elusive truth, since most everyone knew it was so. While there were a number of factors that made Obama electable, the ultimate key to his appeal was that, by virtue of how he looked and spoke and his nice-guy-next-door demeanor, he put whites immediately at ease; for his presentation (as well as the apparent moderation of his views) seemed to reflect their own habits, attitudes and values. Indeed, for many whites, and not only those on the left, Obama appeared virtually a one-man answer to America's intractable race problem. This was not another racism-obsessed, blame whitey black pol whose schtick left white people feeling uncomfortable and guilty, but someone who'd moved beyond all that: a black leader who, in his reasonableness and familiarity, seemed also the ideal representative black man.

"That's a storybook, man."

So, this once Eugene Robinson actually had it exactly right; Obama *did* fit "white America's notion of how a black person should come across." And, *yes*, to say so was an implicit, if unintended, indictment of the millions of blacks who fail to measure up to white middle-class America's idea of "articulate and bright and clean and nice looking," or who speak in "Negro dialect" all the time and not merely when they cynically choose to.

Little wonder that at the outset of his campaign so many black people themselves wondered about his "authenticity," including the archetype of the older brand of black presidential candidate, Jesse Jackson. Watching Obama move from triumph to triumph with mounting resentment and envy, the veteran race hustler finally betrayed his feelings before an open mic, snarling "I'd like to cut his balls off." He apologized for that, but later, when the candidate failed to inject himself into a racial controversy in Jena, Louisiana, Jackson let loose with a remark even more damning. Obama, he declared, is "acting white."

Needless to say, for Jackson and many in his longtime constituency, such a charge, with its ominous suggestion of race betrayal, is as hurtful as they come; and for him to see the younger man succeed by turning it, as he saw it, into a campaign strategy must have been painful almost beyond endurance, signaling as it did his own permanent irrelevance.

But for many ordinary blacks, too, and especially those who feel themselves trapped in the nation's inner cities with little hope of escape, watching Obama's irresistible rise had to be the very definition of cognitive dissonance. For even as the initial sense of disbelief gave way to mounting euphoria, there was the quiet understanding that such a thing was possible only because Obama's were the habits and the values of the white mainstream, not their own; and, indeed, that for this son of Kansan- and East African-born parents and polished product of the faculty lounge, any seeming attachment to black American culture was little more than a useful affectation. In that sense, his wife, who said "for the first time in my adult life, I am proud of my country," may have been his most essential asset.

Well-meaning white people are continually surprised by the hostility with which so many inner-city blacks regard not only the white world but other blacks who, in embracing its values, they regard as having turned their backs on their own. There was no more vivid example than the comments of former NBA star Jalen Rose. A product of Detroit's inner city, in his college days Rose was one of University of Michigan's fabled Fab Five, a gifted if erratic quintet who played the game with the improvisational panache they'd learned in the streets.

Now an ESPN commentator, in 2011 Rose produced a documentary about the group in which he gave vent to his feelings about their old archrivals, the far more disciplined—and successful—Duke teams of the early nineties. "I hated Duke and I hated everything I felt Duke stood for," he said. "Schools like Duke didn't recruit players like me. I felt like they only recruited black players that were Uncle Toms."

He elaborated later: "Certain schools recruit a typical kind of player whether the world admits it or not. And Duke is one of those schools. They recruit black players from polished families, accomplished families."

The player who was most directly targeted by Rose and his ex-teammates was former Duke star Grant Hill, the son of the onetime football star Calvin Hill. Grant went on to enjoy great success in the pros, and his response to Rose in a *New York Times* op-ed surely hit a nerve. "In his garbled but sweeping comment that Duke recruits only black players that were 'Uncle Toms,'" Hill wrote, "Jalen seems to change the usual meaning of those very vitriolic words into his own meaning, i.e., blacks from two-parent, middle-class families. . . . I am beyond fortunate to have two parents who are still working well into their 60s. They received great educations and use them every day. My parents taught me a personal ethic I try to live by and pass on to my children.

"I come from a strong legacy of black Americans. My namesake, Henry Hill, my father's father, was a day laborer in Baltimore. He could not read or write until he was taught to do so by my grandmother. His first present to my dad was a set of encyclopedias, which I now have. He wanted his only child, my father, to have a good education, so he made numerous sacrifices to see that he got an education, including attending Yale."

This was more than simply a personal defense, it was a defense of an optimistic, success-oriented worldview that too many others in the black community scorn as white. Not incidentally, it informs the highly effective, team-oriented playing style for which Duke, under legendary coach Mike Krzyzewski, has long been renowned; a style that enabled Hill's team to beat Michigan's Fab Five every time they met.

"Coach K recruited kids who had every intention of staying in school for four years [and] who had a good chance of competing academically at Duke," the always-thoughtful Jason Whitlock of ESPN and Fox Sports observed. Whitlock was drawing a sharp contrast to the Fab Five, who "stated it was their intention to win a national championship and turn pro as a group after their sophomore season"; and who, with their "baggy shorts, black socks, bald heads and trash talk," represented "the cutting edge of America's unashamed embrace of style over substance."

It almost goes without saying that Whitlock is black—it's nearly impossible to envisage a white reporter with the guts to even edge close to such radioactive honesty. In fact, when I searched through the clips on Nexis from the period around Biden's so-called gaffe, I could unearth only one journalist, a certain Rose Russell of Ohio's *Toledo Blade*, willing to acknowledge that the future vice president basically had it right. In a piece titled "What Was Biden Really Saying?" she pointed out that what was most "revealing about Mr. Biden's remarks, is what he didn't say," which is that Obama "is non-threatening," that he "does not trumpet causes that are solely and specifically of interest to black Americans" and that he is not always looking to "recognize and uncover covert racism."

As for political types, the only one willing to say the same thing was a man readily (and rightly) dismissed as irrelevant. "He wants to show that he is not another politically threatening African-American politician," said Ralph Nader scornfully of Obama's Caucasian-tinged self-presentation. "He wants to appeal to white guilt. You appeal to white guilt not by coming on as black is beautiful, black is powerful. Basically he's coming on as someone who's not going to threaten the white power structure. . . . And they love it. Whites just eat it up."

The anger of Jalen Rose and so many others like him is at least comprehensible, a mix of defensiveness and frustration at belonging to a culture that seems to so profoundly disadvantage those born into it. And, in any case, Rose—who has launched a promising charter school in inner city Detroit— had the good grace to apologize, terming his earlier remarks "ignorant." What's Nader's excuse for ending up in the camp that sees American society as so oppressive and corrupt that it owes blacks and other minorities special privileges in perpetuity and exemption from even well-meant criticism for chronic failure? Such a vision is not just sadly stunted but self-defeating.

Here's the truth: Far from the put-down it has been in the black community, "acting white" is the way people of every ethnic background get ahead in America.

This is confirmed by the entirety of American experience. Successive generations of immigrants have aspired to joining the American mainstream, but doing so meant mastering a specific set of behaviors and values and traditions. My own Jewish immigrant grandparents could never quite make it, still unable to speak more than pidgin English when they died and otherwise excluded from vast swaths of American life by their distance from prevailing cultural norms. But their children all spoke and wrote fluently, and were as versed in American history and literature as any Mayflower descendant, and they got college educations and good jobs; and it was the same for millions of others from every part of the globe, and tens of millions of their children. Even now they may embrace older ethnic traditions—foods and music, holidays and heroes—but

it is from the uniquely American culture that they draw sustenance and a full sense of belonging.

Henry Hill understood that, and so did his son, Calvin, to
whom he gave that treasured set of encyclopedias; and so does
his son Grant, among numberless others.

But the much lamented divide between the races will close
only when, and if, black people en masse come to that understanding as fully as have those of other cultural backgrounds;
and so leave behind attitudes and behaviors that undermine
the possibilities of academic achievement and life success—in
brief, fully embrace the habits of mind associated with "acting
white," rather than resist and belittle them.

No one has preached this message more fervently, or at
greater personal cost, than Bill Cosby. It was at a May 17, 2004,
awards dinner of the NAACP Legal Defense Fund in Washington, D.C., commemorating the 50th anniversary of the
Supreme Court's *Brown v. Board of Education* decision integrat-
ing the nation's schools, that Cosby first generated headlines
in this regard. Addressing an audience that doubtless expected
the sort of entertaining fluff generally associated with celebrity
speakers, he instead delivered a blistering attack on the chronic
failures of the black underclass. "The lower economic people
are not holding up their end in this deal," he proclaimed, proceeding to a long bill of particulars. He derided "black English" and, by implication, those who defended it rather than
insist poor black kids master standard English: "I can't even
talk the way these people talk: 'Why you ain't,' 'Where you
is.' . . . You can't be a doctor with that kind of crap coming out
of your mouth!" He went off on those who dared suggest black
criminality was justified by poverty or racism: "These are not
political criminals. These are people going around stealing
Coca-Cola. People getting shot in the back of the head over a
piece of pound cake and then we run out and we are outraged,

[saying] 'The cops shouldn't have shot him.' What the hell was he doing with the pound cake in his hand?" Nor was he about to let black parents off the hook: "These people are not parenting. They are buying things for kids—$500 for sneakers for what? And won't spend $200 for Hooked on Phonics." Above all, he stressed the value of education, and the failure of black kids to seize the opportunities so readily at hand. As he put it in a follow-up speech in Richmond: "Study. That's all. It's not tough. You're not picking cotton. You're not picking up the trash. You're not washing windows. You sit down. You read. You develop your brain."

Those familiar with the particulars of Cosby's long and hugely successful career were perhaps not as surprised by his trumpeting such views as they might have been had they come from, say, Danny Glover or Stevie Wonder. Cosby had long been not just a pioneer, but a pioneer of a particular kind. For instance, playing Alexander Scott on *On Spy*, which debuted in 1965, Cosby was the first black to star in a conventional action series; but what's less known is that, at Cosby's insistence, race was a total non-issue in the show. His character was in fact the equal of Robert Culp's Kelly Robinson in every respect, except one: as a multilingual Rhodes Scholar, Alexander was smarter. As Culp observed in the commentary accompanying the show's release on DVD, "Our statement is a non-statement."

When Cosby's legendary sitcom debuted 19 years later, race was again deliberately downplayed. Indeed, *The Cosby Show*'s depiction of a loving but complicated family contending with the pressures of contemporary life and popular culture became a phenomenon precisely because it struck so many universal chords. Easygoing as he was in many respects, Cosby's Dr. Cliff Huxtable was (comically) serious in the ways that counted; and had high expectations for both his children and himself.

The relationship between Cosby's Dr. Cliff Huxtable and his son, Theo, especially registered with viewers. The template was established in the show's pilot episode, when the slacker Theo brings home a report card with four D's. His wife is furious, but Cliff decides that rather than berate the boy, he'll teach him a lesson in basic economics. Using Monopoly money, he demonstrates how hard it will be, without an education, to get by on the salary he'd earn in a dead-end job.

Unconvinced, Theo comes back at his father with the sort of heartfelt speech familiar to sitcom viewers. "You're a doctor and mom's a lawyer and you're both successful and everything, and that's great," he offers with genuine sincerity. "But maybe I was born to be a regular person, and have a regular life. If you weren't a doctor, I wouldn't love you less, because you're my dad. And so instead of acting disappointed because I'm not like you, maybe you could just accept me for who I am and love me anyway, because I'm your son."

The show was shot before a live audience, conditioned by exposure to other shows, and this soliloquy, rich with the contemporary ideal of non-judgment, brought on sustained applause. But Cosby's Huxtable sits there a long moment, reflecting on his son's words, evidently chastened. "Theo," he finally replies, "that is the *dumbest* thing I've ever heard in my life."

The shocked laugh lasts a full 10 seconds, as Cosby/Cliff rages on. "No wonder you get D's in everything! Now you are afraid to try, because you're afraid your brain's going to explode and it's going to ooze out of your ears. Now I'm telling you you're going to try as hard as you can. And you're going to do it because I said so. I am your father. I brought you into this world and I'll take you out!"

No one had ever seen such a father before on a sitcom.

Cosby's emphasis on education was rooted in his own past. Raised in Philadelphia, the son of a military man and a maid, he started out far more Theo than Cliff. Though a gifted athlete, with college scholarships looming, he was so indifferent a student that he flunked 10th grade and dropped out. Only after serving four years as a Navy hospital corpsman did he earn his equivalency diploma and attend Temple University on a track and field scholarship.

Subsequently, his respect for education was such that at the height of his celebrity, he returned to school at the University of Massachusetts and got a Ph.D. in education to go with his multiple honorary degrees.

What is largely unknown, or at least little recalled, is that at its inception in the eighties, *The Cosby Show*—today so beloved that Katie Couric suggests "a Muslim version" be launched to help benighted Americans overcome fear "of things they don't understand"—was widely attacked for featuring, as Cosby himself put it, "a white family in blackface." Liberal white journalists in particular, as the distinguished black columnist William Raspberry recalled at the end of the show's run, "were all over the show for its alleged indifference to the black poor," adding that the show's advisor, Harvard psychiatrist Alvin Poussaint, "quickly grew sick of the calls from reporters demanding to know whether the show was black enough. Where were the drugs? The police encounters? The poverty, the rats and roaches and all those so authentically black staples?" Typical was a piece in the *Village Voice* that dismissed the Huxtables as "not black in anything but their skin color. I don't mean just in their lifestyle, even their cultural background, and their whole context of reference, is that of American Caucasians . . . [Cosby] no longer qualifies as black enough to be an Uncle Tom."

In fact, among the many notable things about the *Cosby Show* was how routinely, if subtly, it drew attention to elements of black culture that elevate and ennoble; for even as its protagonist decried sloth, irresponsibility, incivility and excuse making—by anyone—his tastes in music and art reflected his origins. The Huxtables listened to quality jazz and R&B; subplots involved Dizzy Gillespie and Stevie Wonder; and Cliff offhandedly quoted Richard Wright or Langston Hughes. Even the set of the Huxtable living room was adorned with paintings by black artist Varnette Honeywood.

But what the show determinedly did *not* do was conflate black authenticity with a rejection of the American mainstream. And the notion that doing so would be constructive or healthy is just further evidence of the self-sabotaging pathologies that continue to have a stranglehold on too many in the black community.

When Cosby took on those pathologies in what became known as the Pound Cake Speech, it would be reasonable to assume the predominant reaction among blacks was outrage. And, to be sure, there was plenty of that. Some black columnists came forth with "blaming the victim" columns. "Sometimes beating up on defenseless people is just being a bully," wrote Eugene Kane in the *Milwaukee Journal Sentinel*. Observed William Raspberry: "These parents—often single mothers—mostly don't know how to exert effective discipline, and they lack the wherewithal to relocate to a part of town where such discipline may be easier." Then there was Ta-Nehisi Coates in the ever-reliable *Village Voice*, who opined that Cosby "had no solutions . . . so he fell back on what elitists do best—impose condescending lessons on ethics and etiquette. . . . Maybe we are everything the racists say we are—dumb, fat and cute, in a really ugly and childish sort of way. But if we could just pay attention in school, stop stealing, learn proper English, and correctly apply deodor-ant, we'd be all right. Well, maybe not all right, but at least we wouldn't make Cosby look so bad."

In that same spirit, there emerged voices in the black aca-demic elite challenging Cosby's very premises—which is to say, defending and justifying those elements of black culture most rational souls readily identify as destructive. The loudest and most unpleasant of these surely belonged to sociology profes-sor Eric Michael Dyson, currently of Georgetown. Dyson, who gets a lot of face time on cable stations, wrote an entire book answering Cosby in detail and lambasting the entertainer as an all-around sellout. He takes particular umbrage at his "poisonous view" of inner-city youth. For instance, to Cosby's complaint about kids who "wear pants down to the crack"—a supposed fashion statement that had its genesis in the nation's prisons—Dyson scornfully replies that this is "sympathy dress . . . a way of reclaiming the body of a loved one from its demobilized confinement and granting it, vicariously, the free-dom to walk on streets from which it has been removed."

While Dyson doesn't quite excuse black crime, he certainly understands it, tossing out the usual stuff about "an unjust criminal justice system that targets black men with vicious regularity" and blacks "robbed of social standing and personal dignity by poverty and racial injustice." As for Cosby's imagi-nary pound cake thief, in Dyson's view his real problem is that he lives in a society that fails to "train him to cook rather than incarcerate him because he stole when he was hungry."

Dyson goes on to defend the teaching of Ebonics as a legitimate enterprise. "Black English captures the beautiful cadences, sensuous tones, kinetic rhythms, forensic articu-lations, and idiosyncrasies of expression that form the black vernacular voice," he rhapsodizes. "To say 'I am going' is one thing, suggesting a present activity; but to say 'I be going' in

Black English is something else, suggesting a habitual practice, a repeated action."

That being able to speak properly has everything to do with upward mobility is so obvious the point needs no belaboring. As Henry Higgins puts it musically to the aristocratic Pickering as they eye bedraggled Cockney flower girl Eliza Doolittle in *My Fair Lady*'s opening scene: "If you spoke as she does, sir, instead of the way you do, Why, you might be selling flowers, too!"

At least Eliza had what passed for a normal name. Dyson also argues that all those curious black ones—Zohnitha, La Domona, Zanquisha, as well as Formica, Moet, Lexus and others lifted from commercial products—are rooted in black cultural naming tradition, and therefore ought not to be looked at askance.

Recently I ran across a story on the Internet about a young child whose name is spelled "Le-a" who "attends a school in Kansas City, Mo." It could be apocryphal—but, then again, it's so plausible sounding that maybe not. When the teacher asked her mother if it was pronounced Leah or Lay-a., she replied "Ledasha—the dash don't be silent."

While Dyson acknowledges that such names can sometimes be "burdensome" to those forced to tote them around through life, he identifies the real issue here as—what else?—racism, citing a study that showed that job applicants with names like Brad or Laurie were far more likely to get a callback than those named Rasheed or Latonya.

This is no doubt so. But has it truly not occurred to him that employers in serious, profit-making enterprises might be leery of hiring an employee apt to say 'I be going'?

Cosby himself said it better than anyone: "These people are fighting hard to be ignorant."

Far from backing off in the face of criticism, in the wake of his initial salvo Cosby began speaking directly to black audiences across the country, in churches, school auditoriums and before elite gatherings, expanding on his theme. If it was his celebrity—and history—that gave him a certain degree of immunity against the charge of racial treachery, it was also the case that his message resonated powerfully with ordinary black people. NAACP's Kweisi Mfume, for one, observed that he'd heard the same points made by black barbershop philosophers for years.

This gave cover even for the most timorous white liberals to join in, grateful to be able, this once, to speak hard, obvious truths about the black underclass (if only by quoting Bill Cosby) without being pegged as racists or, pretty much the same thing, conservatives. Little wonder that just a couple of months after the Pound Cake Speech, the keynote speaker at the Democratic National Convention in Boston, a still-obscure Illinois Senate candidate named Barack Obama, who's always known where his bread is buttered, said the identical thing. "Go into any inner-city neighborhood, and folks will tell you that government alone can't teach our kids to learn," he intoned, to rapturous approval. "They know that parents have to teach, that children can't achieve unless we raise their expectations and turn off the television set and eradicate the slander that says a black youth with a book is acting white."

Or, to put it in terms that Obama's liberal listeners might have found less congenial, lots of black inner-city folks actually *want* their kids to act white, because they understand full well the term is code for an entire constellation of manners and mores likely to bring success in the mainstream culture; and with it, more than just lip service to full acceptance as equals.

Indeed, overwhelmingly, black people dismissed excuse makers like Dyson to side with Cosby. According to a 2007 Pew survey, 85 percent of blacks deemed the comedian a "good influence" on their community, surpassing then-candidate Obama (76 percent) and trailing only Oprah Winfrey (87 percent).

Eventually, even Ta-Nehisi Coates, the journalist who'd penned the attack on Cosby in the *Village Voice* after the Pound Cake Speech, came around. Cosby's message "played well in black barbershops, churches and backyard barbecues, where a unique brand of conservatism still runs strong," he confessed in a brave and thoughtful piece in the *Atlantic* in 2008. "Outsiders may have heard haranguing in Cosby's language and tone. But much of black America heard instead the possibility of changing their communities without having to wait on the consciences and attention spans of policymakers who might not have their interests at heart." He added that after his father, a former Black Panther, read his assault on the comedian in the *Voice*, "he upbraided me for attacking what he saw as a message of black empowerment."

Of course, there is a considerable distance between recognizing the value of Cosby's tough love advice and a serious, ongoing commitment to the massive cultural shifts it implies. In this sense, the analogy with the immigrants who left behind key parts of their cultures to join the American mainstream is inexact. For one thing, many of these needed no instruction in the surpassing value of education; for another, most arrived when the forebears of today's blacks had already long been on these shores, which makes the continuing failure of blacks to achieve social and economic parity uniquely humiliating; and, so, provokes especially heightened levels of defensiveness.

One would think, for instance, that the notion of getting the most at-risk, black, inner-city kids away from their toxic environment before the most destructive pathologies took hold—from a callousness about fellow human beings to the propensity for violence that is so often the result—would be something policymakers might look at. After all, the idea has a pedigree, and a record of success, stretching back to the 1850s, when the Children's Aid Society began taking feral children who roamed the streets of New York, abandoned and homeless, and transporting them to the Midwest to be adopted, and civilized, by farm families. While some of the estimated 200,000 who rode the so-called orphan trains over the program's 75-year history were exploited as cheap labor, and others in far worse ways, the record shows that the overwhelming majority emerged as productive citizens.

Yet as Newt Gingrich's much-derided orphanage proposal in the nineties confirms, no such program or its contemporary equivalent could ever receive serious consideration today. Even so seemingly humane a concept as facilitating the adoption of black children by white parents is undermined by activists decrying the loss of "cultural identity" black children would suffer at the hands of white adoptive parents. "Culture is the essence of being human," as the National Association of Black Social Workers policy statement on the issue has it. "Culture is second nature. It is a person's values, beliefs, learnings, practices and understandings that are passed on. Children removed from their home, school, religious environment, physicians, friends and families are disengaged from their cultural background. They are denied the opportunity for optimal development and functioning." In fact, the group actually argues that keeping black kids in foster care their entire childhood is preferable to condemning them to life in white suburban homes. As we have seen, their tragic loss has been the gain of kids from China and Peru.

The defensiveness is understandable. Way back in 1897, W.E.B. Du Bois argued that black people have a "double consciousness," which makes them acutely attuned to how they are perceived by whites, and so are "always looking at one's self through the eyes of others, of measuring one's soul by the tape of a world that looks on in amused contempt and pity."

Today, almost as much as then, this is a tremendous obstacle to overcome. But Cosby has it right: It must start with truth telling. And, fortunately, thanks to him and a growing cadre of others, there is a lot more of that going on these days than would once have seemed possible.

Even a handful of liberal black politicians have gotten in on the act. Cory Booker, the charismatic, Stanford-educated mayor of Newark, New Jersey, often cited as one of America's worst cities, has fully embraced what might be called Cosby-style urban governance, angering many in the city's ineffectual and corrupt black old guard by hiring exclusively on the basis of merit, color be damned; in one debate, he shocked liberal observers by actually mocking an opponent's poor command of English. Philadelphia Mayor Michael A. Nutter, meanwhile, has gone out of his way to remind his city's young of the best way to *not* get ahead in modern America. "If you walk into somebody's office with your hair uncombed and a pick in the back, and your shoes untied, and your pants half down, tattoos up and down your arms and on your neck, and you wonder why somebody won't hire you? They don't hire you 'cause you look like you're crazy."

I remember sitting in an integrated audience some years back watching the movie *Barbershop*, and being aware of the whoops of joy from blacks—and the much more tentative laughter from whites—when the crusty old black barber played by Cedric the Entertainer came forth with "the three things that black people need to tell the truth about. Number one:

Rodney King should've gotten his ass beat for being drunk in a Honda in a white part of Los Angeles. Number two: O.J. did it! And number three: Rosa Parks didn't do nuthin' but sit her black ass down!"

Indeed, that Bill Cosby emerged to launch this crusade is not really anomalous, because for some time it has been black comedians—most notably, Richard Pryor, Eddie Murphy, Chris Rock—who have been among the nation's most forthright commentators on race. Though he was too infrequently acknowledged as such, TV's most worthy successor to *The Cosby Show* was the eponymous sitcom of the very funny Bernie Mac. Running from 2001–06, the *Bernie Mac Show* featured the late Mac as a successful comedian who takes his drug-addled sister's three inner-city Chicago kids into his suburban home. They're a difficult bunch, unused to authority or structure, making for a genuine culture clash within the home; but Mac and his wife take on the frustrating task, and in the process of clueing them in about character and values, provided the richest sort of comedy, the kind directly drawn from life.

There's more of the same from Mac's old comedic sidekick, Cedric, who in his standup act actually sends up the whole business of double consciousness. Moving seamlessly from Ebonics-spouting street types to characters who sound like the whitest of effete intellectuals, he demonstrates an astonishing command of every stratum of American society. There's no defensiveness here, but a man utterly comfortable in his skin—and, incidentally, getting rich in the process.

As Joe Biden might say, "I mean, that's a storybook, man."

BLACK
CONSERVATIVES
THE HEROES—AND HOPE—
OF OUR TIME

Since it is "progressive" academics who generally get to write the history books that end up in the nation's classrooms, Herman Cain's surprisingly strong early run for the 2012 Republican presidential nomination will likely receive scant attention in those volumes; noted, if at all, as one of the curiosities of an unusually volatile election season. Indeed, even as the hitherto unknown Cain was confounding the "experts" in the fall of 2011 with his surge to the top of several national polls, liberals were dismissing his rise as a meaningless aberration—or worse. "Herman Cain is probably well liked by some of the Republicans because it hides the racist elements of the Republican party," as Janeane Garofalo observed to a highly receptive Keith Olbermann, adding that "Cain provides this great opportunity so you can say, 'Look, this is not a racist, anti-immigrant, anti-female, anti-gay movement. Look, we have a black man.'"

While it is certainly true that even on the left few are given to such public displays of smug vileness as Garofalo and Olbermann, such a view reflected the thinking of millions on their end of the political spectrum. After all, the very essence of the left/liberal narrative on race is that liberals are decent and generous spirited and their conservative foes are intolerant and small minded, longing to "turn back the clock" to a time when minorities and women and gays knew their place.

Since such a ludicrous fiction so obviously flies in the face of reality, maintaining it is no easy task. And never was this more true than during the brief ascendancy of Herman Cain, when by every measure he was momentarily the favorite of conservatives nationwide. Indeed, for a little while there, most every conservative I know was excited by the successful businessman/non-politician Cain, and, not once, did I hear any of them mention race as even an ancillary reason. What appealed to them was his no-nonsense pro-capitalist message, delivered with unaffected good humor; and, perhaps even more, his passionate love of country, grounded as in was in personal experience. His was the ultimate American success story—the son of a janitor and a cleaning lady who, understanding that getting ahead in a free society was a matter of hard work and perseverance, rose to the very top of his field; and so, along the way, came to despise the welfare state mentality that punishes success and stymies individual initiative. "One of the most important lessons Dad taught us was not to feel like victims," he wrote in his book, released in the heat of the campaign. "He never felt like a victim; he never talked like a victim. And both of our parents taught us not to think that the government owed us something. They didn't teach us to be mad at this country." In the felicitous phrase of Wesley Pruden, editor emeritus of the *Washington Times*, himself caught up in the enthusiasm of the moment, Cain "sings the music of America, and he knows all the words."

Yet this is precisely what made Cain such a mortal threat to the Democratic party and its allies among the cultural elite: He embodied a stark alternative to the entitlement culture that has bought black electoral loyalty—and innumerable elections— even as it has subsidized black dependency and despair. During Cain's rise, it was speculated that, were he to pull off the near-impossible and actually win the nomination, he might pull fully a quarter of the black vote—and even that figure might have been low. At the very least, it is certain a Cain candidacy would have placed the Democratic lock on the black vote at unprecedented risk, along the way opening up untold millions of eyes to his message.

In large measure, this understanding is why, when charges of Cain's sexual improprieties began to emerge, so many conservatives suspected the media of seeking to deliberately sabotage his campaign; knowing liberals—and the liberal media—they had every reason to suspect they would stop at nothing to bring him down. "Herman Cain is the polar opposite of Bill Clinton to these people," conservative media critic Brent Bozell aptly observed. "Political reporters consider him an under-educated buffoon and, as a black conservative, possibly self-loathing to boot. So there are no reasons to delay adultery charges. In fact, they should be rushed on the air, followed by sneering political death notices."

That the Cain campaign ultimately collapsed (equally a casualty of the candidate's all-too-evident inexperience in the policy realm), clearly gave liberals everywhere great satisfaction. But if they were something they are not, wise, they would also take Cain's moment in the spotlight as a warning. For it signaled that, delivered by the right messenger, his message—"I don't believe racism in this country today holds anybody back in a big way"—has the power to undercut the victim mentality that has so long consigned millions to hopelessness and despair.

Indeed, it is a lesson more than a few others have been learning on their own in recent years—the reason the ranks of conservative blacks, while still small, have been steadily growing.

"I found it amazingly easy to get on welfare and simply live off the system," black preacher and commentator Jesse Lee Petersen recalls of the liberals' well intentioned but soul killing handiwork that sent him moving to the right. "I signed up in Los Angeles and started receiving $300 a month. In addition, the system paid my rent and supplied me with food stamps, free medical coverage, and other benefits. I was making the white man pay me back for all the oppression I thought I'd been subjected to in the past. So I partied with that money, caroused with women, and lived a fairly degenerate life."

Self-described former welfare queen Star Parker, one of the most charismatic of today's black conservatives, tells an almost identical story. "On the form they made sure you didn't work, you didn't save and you didn't get married," she says, seemingly still amazed by the sheer lunacy of it all. "And for that you got two checks every month, on the first and fifteenth. Food stamps, too, and all your medical expenses. And day care for your kids, so I could hang out at Venice Beach all afternoon. Why work? It's so much easier to take than to work."

Parker counts herself as having been saved by welfare reform, which nudged her toward personal responsibility and what writer Daniel Akst rightly describes as "the aristocracy of self control."

"Many U.S. Blacks Moving to South, Reversing Trend," the ever-so-carefully-neutral headline over the *New York Times*

March 24, 2011 story had it. Based on newly released census data, the piece detailed the "surprising" revelation that black people in unprecedented numbers have been leaving deep blue states for those of the former Confederacy "as younger and more educated black residents move out of declining cities in the Northeast and Midwest in search of better opportunities."

Given the *Times'* own role as chief mouthpiece for establishment liberalism (and its increasingly pronounced penchant for selective honesty), it is sad but no longer surprising that the paper failed to tell the vital story behind the story. But others were all too happy to help them out. 'Blacks Flee Blue Urban Hells,' a blogger at one conservative website noted. And writing in the *American Interest*, Bard College professor Walter Russell Mead, a Democrat and Obama voter, was among those providing essential context. In fleeing "the stagnant job opportunities, high taxes and rotten social conditions of the mostly blue Northern states," he writes, this horde of internal émigrés has exposed as not just hollow but ultimately destructive the supposedly humane model of liberal governance. The "failure of blue social policy to create an environment which works for Blacks is the most devastating possible indictment of the 20th century liberal enterprise in the United States," he notes, adding ". . . The Census tells us that in the eyes of those who know best, these well intentioned efforts failed. Instead of heaven, we have hell across America's inner cities."

Yet, of course, what baffles many conservatives is that, even as blacks are, in Mead's words, "betting in massive numbers that Southern Republicans will do a better job of helping their kids get good educations, police their communities more fairly" and otherwise "voting red with their feet," they "still vote blue at the ballot box." Indeed, when the aforementioned Star Parker ran for Congress in 2010 as a Tea Party Republican against an ethically challenged black incumbent in California's three-quarters minority 37th District, she polled a mere 22.7%; and precious little of that came from her fellow blacks.

Why the disconnect? Because it is a matter of tradition, culture and unwavering faith among black people that Democrats are on their side and Republicans emphatically are not. Which is to say, it has nothing to do logic or reality. As Milton Himmelfarb famously said of his fellow Jews, they "earn like Episcopalians and vote like Puerto Ricans." It is something tribal and beyond the reach of reason.

So deeply embedded among both Jews and blacks is the idea that liberals represent the forces of light and conservatives all-consuming darkness that, as Norman Pohoretz and others have pointed out, it has long since taken on the dimension of religious conviction.

In fact, the loathing of conservatives is even more pronounced among blacks than Jews—and so, too, is the fear they generate; a product of the assiduously cultivated notion that, more than simply mean spirited and beholden to the rich, conservatives pose an existential threat. In such a worldview, those urging the curtailment of ineffective government programs or affirmative action are not arguing for more effective governance or individual equity, they are unapologetic heirs to the bigots of the discredited old order.

Indeed, for millions of black people, marinated in the ideology of victimhood and dependence, the possibility that the conservative path might actually offer a better approach to the persistent problems plaguing the underclass is literally beyond imagination.

Moreover, where hostility toward the right and its program is far less pronounced among observant Jews than among the rigorously secular (for whom ideological engagement serves as an alternative belief system), in the black community such hostility cuts across class and denominational lines. In December

2010, when the Conference of National Black Churches, comprising nine black denominations with a combined membership of over 30 million, was formed "to improve the quality of life for African Americans," the press releases emanating from its founding conference told the sadly familiar story. Full of the familiar buzzwords about "advocacy" on behalf of "social justice," they included not a syllable about the myriad government policies that undercut independence and initiative or the forty million black children consigned to homes without fathers. To the contrary, in a joint letter, the pastors of the nine denominations condemned the Bush-era tax cuts, calling it "utterly shameful that those who insisted that the deficit be reduced, now celebrate billions of dollars being added to the deficit as tax cuts for the wealthy."

It is their willingness to take on that entrenched mentality that makes black conservatives not just brave, but vitally important. Indeed, their philosophical grit, buttressed (as in Cain's case) by personal experience, renders them uniquely positioned to take on the most dangerous argument of all: that in its well-meant efforts at inclusivity and cultural understanding, America's elites have legitimized, and mainstreamed, black underclass attitudes and behaviors—from the casual acceptance of single parenthood to the embrace of dependence over self reliance—once universally understood to be aberrant and destructive, in the process fundamentally transforming the larger culture itself for the worse. Proverbial voices in the wilderness, principled conservative blacks are, far more, intrepid pathfinders, charting a different and better course for others less audacious and thoughtful.

Of course, thoughtful audacity was a trait once widely ascribed to Barack Hussein Obama. But even many of his former acolytes soon came to grasp that, for all the rhetoric, at his essence he was the same old-same old in a glossier package.

In fact, Obama is truly the ultimate beneficiary of affirmative action; a man whose only obvious qualification for the office of President of the United States was the color of his skin. "How," Matt Peterson asked in a potent September, 2011 piece in The American Thinker, as Obama's dangerous unfitness for the job was becoming all-too-manifest, "did a man so devoid of professional accomplishment beguile so many into thinking he could manage the world's largest economy, direct the world's most powerful military, execute the world's most consequential job?" The answer, alas, is that so desperately did they wish him to be as brilliant and far-seeing as they hoped, they willfully ignored all evidence to the contrary—or, in the case of his media acolytes, adamantly refused to ferret it out. True enough, there was huge idealism in this, the conviction that in the golden voiced Obama, America was at last fully living up to its best self. Yet for those willing to see, it was always a fiction. As Peterson notes with pitiless straightforwardness, given what we knew of the man's history, Obama appears to have been boosted by preferences every step of the way, his ethnicity easing his way into elite colleges and the editorship of the Harvard Law Review, and on through the murky realms of Illinois politics (where he was most notable for voting "present") and into the presidency itself. Has any other candidate in recent times, let alone one with a slew of unsavory associates in his background, ever so fully escaped serious scrutiny? Why, to cite one small but telling fact, have we never even seen Obama's transcripts, where those of George W. Bush and Al Gore were part of the public record from the outset, and Rick Perry's were leaked even before he announced for the presidency? Why, unlike Cain's, were his egregious public lapses—"I've been in 57 states"; claiming a Kansas tornado killed 10 thousand, rather than the actual 12; insisting on the campaign trail that "tiny countries" like Iran don't pose "a serious threat"—glossed over and ignored.

Little wonder that Obama is famously affronted by even the most legitimate criticism; by dint of his racial status he'd almost never been held to account for anything. Little wonder, too, that his impulse under attack is self pity—and to stoke the resentment and sense of ill usage of his followers.

Since it is pretty much a given in black America that every imaginable evil can somehow be ascribed to the same root cause, it is even less of a surprise that so many would ascribe Obama's declining appeal to white racism—never mind that whites gave him more votes in 2008 than were gained by fellow Democrats Al Gore or John Kerry. It yet again only signals the refusal of millions of our fellow citizens to face not only the reality of Barack Obama's situation, but their own.

In the end, the Obama regime, once advertised as holding out enormous promise, will very likely leave in its wake an especially toxic residue of bitterness, with Obama angrily depicted by too many black people as another victim of white America.

And, as always, whites—conservatives almost as much as liberals, Republicans as well as Democrats—will shrink from meaningfully confronting the errant nonsense, for fear of being smeared themselves.

Yet, too, as always, black conservatives can be expected to rise to the challenge. "In black America," the ever insightful Shelby Steele observes of the fight he and others have been waging for so long, "identity has become almost totalitarian . . . You [must] subscribe to the idea that the essence of blackness is grounded in grievance, and if you vary from that you are letting whites off the hook. And we're gonna call you a sell out."

'Sell out' is the least of it. For out and proud black conservatives, especially if they're seen to have influence, dealing with vicious *ad hominen* assaults is a way of life. If group think is always a powerful force, it is enforced with special intensity in the black community, and long before anyone heard of Herman Cain, the admirable likes of Clarence Thomas and Condoleeza Rice were inured to being sneered at as Uncle Toms and Aunt Jemimas, oreos, house niggas, and worse. Nor, needless to say, are activist blacks the only offenders; for their attacks give cover and full absolution to white haters on the left.

Such is the contempt in which conservative blacks are held by the left that even a clear history of fighting racial discrimination offers no protection from the liberal impulse to punish and diminish. Those of a certain age will recall James Meredith, the young man from Kosciusko, Mississippi who in 1962 faced down rioters and multiple death threats to integrate the University of Mississippi. At the time he was rightly lauded as an inspirational figure, and even more so four years later, when he was shot outside Memphis at the head of a civil rights march, prompting Martin Luther King to carry on in his stead. But an Air Force vet and fiercely independent, Meredith always resisted too close an association with mainstream civil rights organizations, declaring of his decision to take on Ole Miss, "Nobody hand picked me. I made the decision myself. I paid my own tuition." So it is not surprising that Meredith eventually emerged as a conservative, declaring "My agenda is to take the power away from the white liberals and give it back to the head of each black family." Less surprising still is that, although this *bona fide* civil rights hero is still around and readily reachable, he is today never heard from in the press. And, speaking of hidden history, who knew that sixties icon Eldridge Cleaver, once an international radical superstar as the most charismatic of the leading Black Panthers, had become by his death in 1998 a conservative Republican? Not me, until I began some serious poking around. Then, again, he's another important figure out of recent history not about to be celebrated during Black History Month.

Bill Cosby's a more complicated case. When he began his heroic campaign for higher standards and honest self evaluation within the black community, many conservatives rushed to embrace him as one of their own. Yet from the outset, Coz has fled from that designation like his life depends on it— which in a public sense, in a time when to be known as a black conservative can be the kiss of death, it perhaps does. When, in the tumultuous aftermath of his Pound Cake Speech, Cosby issued a statement elaborating on his views, he ended it this way: "If I have to make a choice between keeping quiet so that conservative media does not speak negatively or ringing the bell to galvanize those who want change in the lower economic community, then I choose to be a bell ringer."

Where did *that* come from? Keeping silent so that the "conservative media" won't take pleasure and sustenance from his criticism of black people; a conservative media that, alone in the ideological wilderness, had for years been making almost exactly the same arguments about behavior and personal responsibility Cosby was now making and for exactly the same reason; to help black people more fully integrate into the fabric of mainstream life? From the fight for welfare reform (twice vetoed by Bill Clinton before he signed on in his Dick Morris-inspired pre-reelection triangulation push) to the ongoing nationwide battles for school choice (resisted tooth and nail by teachers unions and other liberal special interests), had it not been conservatives pushing precisely those policies that reflect the values he himself now championed? And constantly getting called racist for their trouble?

The most charitable explanation is that such an attack was calculated, since in the varied circles where Cosby runs, from Hollywood to academia to black churches and speakers platforms at NAACP conferences, being suspected of closet conservatism might instantly delegitimize his message.

But, too, such a harsh view of conservatives is unquestionably also a product of his age and background. In his long ago youth it was indeed the Dems, the party of JFK and LBJ, fighting the good fight on civil rights, and back then conservatives were too often on the other side. Mr. Conservative himself, Barry Goldwater, opposed the 1964 Civil Rights Act (if on principled federalism, not racial, grounds); and four years later Richard Nixon pursued a 'Southern strategy' to finally take the White House, along the way bringing a large chunk of the traditionally pro-segregation Southern Democratic bloc, as personified by newly minted Republican Strom Thurmond, into the ranks of the GOP. It is hardly happenstance that in those years nearly as many photos of the Kennedy brothers were to be found in black homes as of Martin Luther King.

At the time, Cosby wasn't much known as an activist, but he was a reliable enough liberal that he was on Nixon's infamous 1973 "Enemies List," showing up at #124, just ahead of Jane Fonda. And, in fact, his politics—even including those touching on race—have in many respects remained unchanged since then, notwithstanding his crusade for personal responsibility. In September 2009, for instance, he took to his Facebook page to endorse Jimmy Carter's noxious view "that racism is playing a role in recent outbursts against President Obama," and to wonder "how many people oppose Obama's (health care) plan because the President is African American?" Two years later, in April 2011, Cosby actually joined Obama and other notables at a bash celebrating the twentieth anniversary of the disgraceful Al Sharpton's National Action Network.

The relative timidity of a bullet-proof figure like Cosby makes the bravery of true black conservatives even more worthy of celebration. Take, for instance, Deneen Borelli, a Fellow with Project 21, a network of black conservatives pushing racial blindness and free market solutions to social problems.

A Tea Party stalwart and a regular on conservative media, she'll have an excellent shot at ending up on *Obama's* enemies list, in the not altogether unlikely event his people are compiling one. "By engaging in race-card politics," she flatly asserts, "Obama shows he is willing to follow the lead of Al Sharpton and Jesse Jackson to ignite racial tension as a means of maintaining power and furthering his agenda. By stooping to this level, Obama is discrediting his position as our nation's leader."

Such outspokenness is typical of today's small but growing band of black conservatives. Numbering activists, pundits and political figures, their fearlessness commands as much admiration among their fellow conservatives as it provokes loathing in their political opponents—and not just loathing, but also its Hunter Thompsonian twin, fear. If indeed they are able to eventually persuade enough of their fellow blacks that, far from agents of compassion, liberals are the architects of the very policies that have consigned millions to dead end lives, the Democrat Party will face electoral oblivion.

More than a political strategy, this is a moral crusade; one, as Paul Ryan said of the debt crisis, "involving questions of principle and purpose . . . A government that would solve problems without limit must necessarily have power without limit to do it." As pundit Michael Walsh notes, "There's nothing humane about a system whose unspoken purpose is to keep people dependent, resentful and impoverished."

Conservative Republican Michael Williams, as head of the Texas Railroad Commission the first black to hold statewide elected executive office in that state's history, speaks for many others in his utter disgust with liberals' indiscriminate use of the race card for political ends. "As an African-American son of the South," he says, "I grew up in a time and place where you didn't have to divine intent or deconstruct code words to find racism . . . We have rid our institutions of government of the practice of discrimination; if only we could rid our political discourse of the ugliness that ensues when we ascribe discriminatory motive to statements with no obvious discriminatory aspect."

The readiness—increasingly, the eagerness—of such people to say such things in the face of withering scorn makes them genuine heroes of our time. In an America where welfare state policies have everywhere eroded the prideful individualism and can-do resilience that sustained this country for the first two hundred years of its existence, their fight to drag their fellow blacks kicking and screaming toward their own self interest is, indeed, a fight for all Americans.

Unquestionably, the most despised black conservative on the contemporary scene is Clarence Thomas, whose entire public career stands as a rebuke to group think. Having come to widespread public notice as a result of an especially contemptible smear by ideological foes desperate to keep him off the High Court, and then defeating it by identifying a former employee's unsubstantiated charges as the attempted "high-tech lynching" that it was, he has gone on to play a key role in establishing the Court's current conservative cast. Even more infuriating to liberals, their ceaseless barrage of *ad hominem* attacks, ranging from run of the mill Uncle Tomism to the charge that he is too stupid to speak up in open court—seem to faze him not at all. And he's still young enough that he stands to give them *agita* for decades to come.

If Thomas is Black Conservative Enemy Number One, not too far down the list has been anti-preferences crusader Ward Connerly, whose work likewise profoundly challenges the victim/dependency mentality. Connerly's public appearances at college auditoriums and town halls routinely send defenders of racial preferences spiraling into paroxysms of rage. "He has no ethnic pride," sneers black California Democrat Diane Watson," in a characteristic attack. "He doesn't want to be black." Mild in manner and unfailingly courteous, Connerly is the sort of old fashioned gentleman who leaps up to pull out the chairs of female opponents like Watson on debating platforms—then calmly destroys them in argument. As he points out, to their infuriated disbelief, it is *they* and the other racial bean counters who practice racism, not those who seek to make racial blindness a matter of law.

Needless to say, many liberals have trouble hearing such a proposition, let alone grasping it, since theirs is a logic that sees racial compassion as measurable in tangibles: guaranteed places in university classrooms and preferences in hiring, larger unemployment checks and more dollars poured into failing school systems. That it might also involve reduced dependence and enhancing dignity and self worth doesn't compute—sometimes even after the case has been made. One will recall the vitriolic rhetoric that preceded passage of welfare reform in 1996. As *City Journal*'s Kay Hymowitz notes, New Jersey senator Frank Lautenberg predicted it would result in " 'children begging for money, children begging for food, eight- and nine-year-old prostitutes.' Ted Kennedy called it 'legislative child abuse.' The *New York Times* called it 'draconian' and 'a sad day for poor children.' 'They are coming for the children,' wailed Congressman John Lewis of Georgia, 'coming for the poor, coming for the sick, the elderly and disabled.' 'What's next?' demanded Congressman William Clay of Missouri, 'Castration?' Peter Edelman, Assistant Secretary for Planning and Evaluation in Clinton's Department of Health and Human Services and husband of Children's Defense Fund founder Marian Wright Edelman, resigned after the welfare bill was signed, then wrote a piece saying it would lead to 'more malnutrition and more crime, increased infant mortality and increased drug and alcohol abuse.' As for the NAACP, a spokesman said the group 'saw this as a throwback to the issue of states' rights, and our history tells us enough about that. It's negative and frightening.'"

So what happened? Welfare reform was a roaring success, reducing the welfare rolls by 2.8 million or nearly 60 percent, with similarly striking decreases in the rates of poverty of single mothers and children. Just as vitally, as Star Parker attests, the linking of welfare to work changed the way many people thought about themselves and their possibilities, thus breaking what had seemed an endless cycle of poverty.

Of course, all this has long since disappeared down the memory hole, and the familiar liberal formulations—"anti-family," "anti-child," "mean-spirited"—continue to be heard in response to every perceived challenge to social welfare policy. Ineffectual and destructive as that agenda so clearly is, it has locked liberals and the underclass into symbiosis; condescending paternalism and pitifully low expectations from one side, perceived helplessness and acceptance of permanent victim status on the other.

Yet in key ways, this has never been a natural alliance. As is often observed, on a number of key social issues—abortion, same sex marriage, even premarital sex—blacks are far closer to Republicans than to their fellow Democrats, especially those in the activist base, whose reflex is to sneer at the very term "traditional values." Indeed, according to a 2008 Gallup poll, fully 76% of black people go to church, an even higher percentage than white Republicans. All this was evident in the enormous support in the black community for Cosby's views— a reaction that caught so many white liberals by surprise.

This is the moral tradition from which most of today's black conservatives emerged. It is striking how often notable members of that fraternity, looking back on why they rejected the victim mind-set that shackles so many others, cite the strength and dignity of forebears. For Herman Cain, as his memoir makes clear, it was his parents. For Clarence Thomas, it was his grandfather, Myers Anderson, in segregated rural Pinpoint, Georgia, who stressed education, faith and moral courage. "The damn vacation is over!" he announced, when young Clarence and his brother arrived to live under his roof, but the boys rose to the challenge. For Ward Connerly, it was his Uncle James, with whom he lived from the age of five, the first black man he'd ever known "who carried himself like a free man." Alternately gruff and good humored, he was never less than independent and unbendingly principled. For Walter Williams, the noted economist (who oddly enough grew up in the same Philadelphia housing project as Bill Cosby), it was his single mother, Catherine, described by Williams' great good friend Tom Sowell as "one of those strong and wise black women who has had much to do with providing the foundation from which many other black men and women rose out of poverty to higher levels of achievement."

Significantly, Williams and Sowell, among a fair number of other prominent black conservatives, started out on the left. "I was more sympathetic to Malcolm X than Martin Luther King because Malcolm X was more of a radical who was willing to confront discrimination in ways that I thought it should be confronted, including perhaps the use of violence," Williams told the *Wall Street Journal's* Jason Riley of his early student years. But then he started studying economics under "tough-minded professors who encouraged me to think with my brain instead of my heart. I learned that you have to evaluate the effects of public policy as opposed to intentions."

For the cynically minded, or simply the practical, there is clearly an opening here. Surely many other black people, steeped in the same tradition, might be similarly inclined to move rightward if granted a fuller understanding of what they'd be embracing and, even more so, what they were leaving behind.

The shooting star that was the Cain campaign is just one of the reasons to believe things are moving steadily in that direction. Black conservatives now appear so regularly on the air, in print and on the web that most every black person in America is at least occasionally exposed to once-verboten messages. The new media is especially subversive in this regard, spreading ideas as dangerous to the racial status quo as are those about freedom in the mullahs' Iran. Articles on conservative websites about the excesses of black culture often have anonymous recent converts posting in droves with stories of their own; some telling of conflicts with family and friends, but many also going on about the joys of personal liberation. Callers to talk radio often say the same thing.

No fewer than 33 blacks, many Tea Partiers, vied for congressional seats in 2010, and two of them were elected: Tim Scott in South Carolina's First Congressional District, who cruised to victory with 65 percent of the vote after routing Strom Thurmond's son in a Republican primary runoff; and tough as nails retired Lieutenant Colonel Allen West, a veteran of Iraq and Afghanistan and an even redder meat conservative, who took Florida's 22nd CD by a comfortable nine points. While neither was elected principally by black voters—Scott's district is 21 percent black, West's only four percent—their victories presented an entirely new model that has clearly offered a pathway to others; not least, Cain. West in particular made it clear from the outset he would be a different kind of black congressman. Under sustained attack from self-styled "civil rights activists," he did what few Republicans before him dared: He counterattacked, hard. Confronted by a slew of outrageous charges, ranging from "extremism" to an alleged "disrespect for women," West went directly after the messenger. "One might wonder—is it open season on a principled black conservative? I wonder what the reaction would have been if I were a Democrat?"

Soon after being sworn in, West joined the Congressional Black Caucus—on the grounds that someone had to directly stand up to this group of purported leaders who reflexively identify racism as the cause of every ill faced by the black community. And stand up to them he did, publicly calling out the despicable Maxine Waters (D-CA) and Barbara Lee (D-CA) as contemporary versions of the "plantation boss" and calling himself a "modern day Harriet Tubman to kind of lead people on the Underground Railroad away from that plantation into a sense of sensibility." Little wonder that, even after having gone to battle against Al Qaeda and the Taliban, West has likely never felt so besieged by enemies as he does in the CBC conference room. But he's kept coming at them. When Waters and Indiana's André Carson smeared the Tea Party in ways venomously irresponsible even for them, fellow CBC-er West was there to call them to account. "I believe it is incumbent on you to both condemn these types of hate-filled comments, and to disassociate the Congressional Black Caucus from these types of remarks," he wrote with admirable understatement to CBC Chairman Emmanuel Cleaver, making for all the world like he was dealing with serious and responsible human beings. "Otherwise I will have to seriously reconsider my membership within the organization."

"Insert laughter," as conservative black commentator Larry Elder observed of this last.

Still, the importance of West and Scott's presence on the Republican side of the aisle can hardly be overstated. Indeed, given their example, it is no coincidence that so many other

black conservatives were encouraged to sign up for the electoral next round.

Accustomed as we are to the old paradigm, it will strike
some as inconceivable that black people might anytime soon
move in significant numbers from Barack Obama's camp toward
that represented by Allen West. Yet, on the evidence, it's not
nearly as far fetched as it seemed only recently. "[B]ack in the
early years, you and I were pretty pessimistic as to whether
what we were writing would make an impact—especially since
the two of us seemed to be the only ones saying what we were
saying," Thomas Sowell wrote not long ago to his old friend
Walter Williams. "Today at least we know that there are lots of
other blacks writing and saying similar things . . . and many of
them are sufficiently younger that we know there will be good
people carrying on the fight after we are gone."

Reminded of his friend's words by Jason Riley, himself
one of the leading lights among today's younger generation
of black journalists, during their conversation for the *Wall
Street Journal*, Williams cautiously agreed. "You find more and
more black people—not enough in my opinion but more and
more—questioning the status quo," he allowed. "When I fill
in for Rush, I get emails from blacks who say they agree with
what I'm saying. And there are a lot of white people questioning ideas on race, too. There's less white guilt out there. It's
progress."

In Barack Obama's approach to many issues, and race in
particular, the contrast with black conservatives casts him in
the worst possible light. Where they are hopeful and forward
looking, he remains very much a man of the past, still seeing
"racism" as the cause of all ills, refusing to take on the hard
fights that need to be fought. His adherents like to say his election was historic, and perhaps it was. But, increasingly, there is

reason to hope its aftermath will prove even more meaningful: the period when black people at last began waking up to the reality that victimization and liberal condescension are dead ends.

AFTERWORD

One gorgeous Saturday in the spring of 2011, in the big city for the day, my wife and I headed over to the Museum of the City of New York to see an exhibit on the Apollo Theater, the legendary Harlem launching pad for so many revered black musicians. The show was fascinating, full of memorabilia involving everyone from Bill "Bojangles" Robinson to Michael Jackson, as well as lots of unexpected stuff, like the original theater owner's confidential notes assessing the drawing power of performers like Lionel Hampton and Billie Holiday.

But we saw something else that also left an impression—and a sour aftertaste. In fact, since you enter the museum through the bookstore, and it was directly ahead, it was apt to be the first thing that caught your eye: a book cover showing a white kid, from behind, his back bare and his underpants tops hitched several inches above his jeans, gangsta style. Its title

221

was *Everything But the Burden*, and the subtitle completed the thought: *What White People Are Taking from Black Culture*.

Since I was well into this book, the timing was fortuitous (if that is the word), for here was something that seemed to sum up much I hoped to say.

A bit of leafing through the book further clarified its point of view, which is, basically, that whites appropriate for themselves everything worthwhile in black culture—"from music to dance, fashion, sports and much more"—and leave behind only the terrible liability (at least in America) of being black. Indeed, so the essays within assert, even the sartorial styles adapted by black prison inmates as a visual cry of defiance against The Man have been taken up by spoiled suburban white kids indifferent to the noble message they were meant to convey.

Why was such a volume so prominently featured in connection with a show celebrating the glorious likes of Ella Fitzgerald and Duke Ellington? Presumably because, in the fevered imagination of some administrator, even the greatest of the black luminaries who starred at the Apollo were victims of this syndrome, allowed to prosper, perhaps, but only at the terrible cost of surrendering their souls. Or something. When it comes to this kind of thinking, logical coherence is rarely front and center.

Still, the distortion of reality in this particular case was especially audacious and offensive. In the vernacular suggested by that photo, it gets everything ass-backward.

Let us count the ways.

Far from having been appropriated by anyone, jazz, soul, and, yes, rap continue to be recognized throughout the world as distinctively black musical forms, and the black artists associated with them are widely celebrated and, in many cases, enormously wealthy. That such music—like other significant black contributions to our common national life—is simultaneously regarded as distinctively *American* is a good thing and to be celebrated, signaling as it does our sense that we are one people and the ultimate irrelevance of skin color.

All blacks get are "the burden"? Like all other Americans, those millions of blacks who avail themselves of the vast bounty on offer to those born in this most upwardly mobile of societies—from educational and professional opportunities to the richness of our shared culture—are among the world's chosen, uniquely positioned for life success. "Thank God that I am an American," veteran *Washington Post* correspondent (and certainly no conservative) Keith Richburg was honest enough to write in 1997, after a stint covering Africa and witnessing firsthand the horrific living conditions and corruption rampant in that continent. Though much attacked for it by his fellow blacks, more than a decade later he held fast that assessment, writing, "I was fortunate that circumstances meant I had been born outside Africa."

Inconceivable as the thought seems to be to the book's contributors, there are major elements of today's black underclass culture—fatherlessness, violence, music that coarsens and demeans and, damn right, gangsta fashion—that the mainstream would be far better off without. To the extent they have been loosed on society at large, and appropriated by the young and witless, it is to the detriment of us all.

Whites who try to make the case otherwise, justifying and even celebrating the worst excesses of urban life in the name of multiculturalism, do black people no favors. Whether smug elitists or just the rigor-deficient well intentioned, their defense of dysfunction is the height of condescension.

Still, that such a volume is displayed so prominently in a venue paid for by tax dollars is just an incidental reminder of the power such people command in modern American life. That they are prepared to use that power to seek to destroy those on the other side by branding them as racist—and to think even better of themselves for doing so—is a fact of contemporary existence.

This is why these have been, and continue to be, such tough fights to make. But thank God there are those out there who know they're worth making. Many of them have been cited in these pages.

So let's end with the individual with whom we began. "I am black and happy to be so," writes the invaluable Shelby Steele, "but my identity is not my master. I'm my master."

ACKNOWLEDGEMENTS

There are many people who deserve credit for the thoughts and attitudes that appear on these pages: all those who, through their own courageous actions, provided the impetus for me to write it. Foremost among them are the black conservatives to whom I devote the concluding chapter. They stand as exemplars of moral courage in a time all too lacking in that most vital of attributes. My colleagues at *City Journal*, the splendid publication of the Manhattan Institute, have long taken the lead in challenging left/liberal orthodoxy on race—and none more consistently or forcefully than Heather Mac Donald. Indeed, Heather has written so compellingly on the subject that, knowing how heavily I would rely on her pioneering work, I sought out her okay before launching into the book. True to form, her only interest was in spreading the word. Among others at *City Journal* who have always been helpful and supportive are the magazine's former editor Myron Magnet, and the current one, Brian Anderson; Stefan Kanfer;

Kay Hymowitz; Steve Malanga; Sol Stern; Fred Siegel and Ben Plotinsky.

There is no finer or more inspiring publisher than Roger Kimball, and his team at Encounter—Lauren Miklos, Heather Ohle, Lesley Rock, Sam Schneider, Nola Tully, Katherine Wong—is beyond first rate.

A number of friends contributed to this book in important ways: Gerry Garibaldi, a gifted writer and educator whom I quote at length; Neil Goldman, Marlene Mieske, Bernie Goldberg; Ron Mitchell; Kim Neiss and David List. Then, too, there are the guys on The Bench—Jerry Kane, Alex Piccirillo, Alex Sneddon, Gray Delany, and Bob Conti—who were a constant source of feedback, and whose advice is never less than invaluable. And Jenny Tripp, who has rendered services beyond the call of duty.

Finally, as always, there's my first and best reader, Priscilla Turner. These acknowledgement pages are always an opportunity to tell her—and remind myself—how glad I am she married me.